Buteo augur Ursula Franke

Encounters with Death

Thomas Bryson and Dr. Ursula Franke-Bryson

NIGHTSKY
PRODUCTIONS

Encounters with Death

Graphic design Thomas Bryson
Photography Thomas Bryson unless otherwise credited.

ISBN 978-3-9815179

Night Sky Productions,
Tal 34 Munich 80331 Germany

tb@thomas-bryson.de
www.ursula-franke.de

NIGHTSKY
PRODUCTIONS

Contents

Foreword

Encounters with Death was written by American author, systemic constellation facilitator and trainer Thomas Bryson, in close collaboration with his German wife and colleague, Dr. Ursula Franke-Bryson. It is published by Night Sky Productions in Munich, Germany in association with Conexão Sistêmica in São Paulo, Brazil. *Encounters with Death* is written primarily as a guide for systemic constellation facilitators, but is appropriate for readers who are interested in applying systemic thinking to their professional practices, who may want to explore the spiritual aspects of death, or those who simply want to expand the context of their world view by exploring the constraints of life and death and the dimension which contains them both. Please feel free to read only those chapters which interest you and to leave the rest. All errors in the text are the sole responsibility of the authors. Please feel free to give comments: tb@thomas-bryson.de.

Gyps africanus Grant Reed Letaka Safaris

Acknowledgments

The author would like to acknowledge all those who have contributed to his understanding of the topic, but there are too many to mention. Nevertheless, I would be remiss without naming and thanking some of the key players: Dr. Reid Bryson for his love, inspiring curiosity, the scale of his world view and for passing on to me his love of the interdisciplinary approach; Claire Levine for her unstinting support, love and patience; Ram Dass and his guru Neem Karoli Baba for awakening my knowledge that through approaching death I would be approaching life; all of my hospice patients for their insights, joys, suffering, beauty, fear, dignity and the reality of their life and passing; Lama Surya Das for the direct seeing of Dzogchen; Calvin Tabata Sensei and the Oregon Ki Society for Aikido with mind and body coordinated; Hanuman Golden for seeing me as I had always longed to see myself; Adyashanti for encouraging me to bring the Dharma into my work; Drs. Lynn Reer and Jane Peterson for introducing me to systemic constellation, as well as all the other practitioners from whom I have learned and grown; Dr. Ursula Franke-Bryson for the depth of her experience, for being my wife, professional partner and mentor; the clients who have trusted and taught me along the way; my colleagues group for providing a strong, safe container for my own personal exploration; to Oswaldo Santucci and Glaucia Paiva in São Paulo for their trust and support.

I, Ursula, want to thank my parents who gave me all of what I am. More and more, I understand my father´s search and hope, and my own. He died when I was on my first big excursion into life, and since then, I have been trying to fathom his life and death and to fulfill his legacy, which is alive in me: to understand and find a peaceful place while being here. And my deepest gratitude is with my husband for holding my heart.

We would both like to thank Doris and Günther Kleemann for providing us with a house in the desert where we can return to the silence of nature and remember our inner silence. And of course, the night sky for her constant companionship.

Chameleon Ursula Franke

Introduction

Better to die now while you still live, than to live now enslaved to fear of death.

Ecclesiastes 9:4-6

The fear of death has its complement in the fear of living. Denying death, is to deny our constant companion in life and to reduce both life's depths and heights. Exploring death and dying enriches one's inner and outer worlds, by adding meaning and the beauty of contrast. Ironically, the vain attempt to avoid the topic of death, limits one's focus to all the potential risks in life, always highlighting what is fearful or dangerous, while inevitably pushing one ever deeper into the corner of resistance and suffering.

As our own actual experience of life and death is always personal and subjective, so is this book. The clinical examples and self-experience exercises contained herein come directly from our clinical practice and are consistent with the classical scientific method: observation, creation of hypotheses, intervention and their verification or falsification by observation.

Encounters with Death includes the gleanings from a life of self-inquiry, including many years of direct experience with death and dying, as well as steeping in the power of presence through Zen meditation. In addition, *Encounters with Death*, is a book about death in systemic constellation psychology and draws on many years of clinical experience in that field, as well as other therapies. This is a practical, yet philosophical guide to approaching the kernel of human psychology - the human conditioning and response to the reality that each of our lives is short and includes the death of ourselves and those whom we love.

Encounters with Death is divided into two parts: Hospice and Systemic Constellation. *Part One: Hospice*, begins with *Death and Dying: Thomas Bryson and Dr. Ursula Franke-Bryson in Conversation*, by way of a personal introduction to Thomas Bryson, his perspective and experience with the topic. It continues with *Stories from the Dying*, eleven accounts of dying patients whom the author encountered in nearly fifteen years of direct care of the dying and their families in the United States. The accounts are not representative or average, and are subject to cultural bias. Each death is one which stood out in the author's experience and is followed by a short commentary.

The first story from the dying is, *It will be exciting!*, describing one woman's life-changing test flight out of her body, and ends with *Kathy*, which includes a description of an after-death visitation by the deceased. *Eight Hours with the Dead*, touches on a daughter's recognition that the most important aspect of her relationship with her mother was unchanged by her mother's death. *Angel Band*, attempts to describe the indescribable moments of a woman's dying while being accompanied by her own personal angel choir. *A Lover of God*, highlights practical spirituality. In the story *Dresden*, concepts from systemic constellation *In the mind's eye*, are used with a man in a coma. *The Marathon* is an account of the death of a long-distance runner. People sometimes wait to die for particular events, such as the arrival of expected visitors or simply permission to go, as is told in *The Ritual. Quieting the Demons*, tells of how the children of a dying man applied ancient skills and were able to accomplish healing beyond the scope of modern medicine. *Brenda's Vision* speaks for itself. *Old Flames* describes a case of physician's assisted suicide with musical accompaniment.

Part Two: Systemic Constellation, also begins with a conversational interview, *Death in Systemic Constellation*, which focuses on how the inherited patterns of death and death avoidance appear in clinical practice and accesses some of the depth of therapeutic experience of co-author Dr. Ursula Franke-Bryson. There is a brief section including five *Self-Experiencing Exercises*, followed by ten *Clinical Examples with Commentary*, which explore death in relation to systemic constellation. The first example, *Reunion in Death*, was done as a Skype session. *Tension in the Neck* describes how a physical symptom echoed past trauma. *Finding Distance* is about the legacy of war and the futility of running from oneself. *I was afraid before that*, is a case of replacing fear with dignity. *At the Station* describes how presence and physical containment changed the dimensions of a taken-over trauma-trance. *Your ancestors are waiting*, describes the lasting resonance which can occur in systemic constellation. *That's my sentence!* is an example of a son tracing a symptom from his own body to his father's wartime experience and relieving it there. Like *Finding Distance*, *Seeking World Peace* expands the dimensions of the context needed for healing. *Losing One's Head* cuts to the point, and finishes with a classic teaching story. The book ends with a highly personal account of the author's own exploration of the legacy of the Native American genocide, simply titled *Horror*.

Theoretic comments and philosophic speculations are spread throughout the text. It was our hope that in the realm of death, which stretches beyond one's mental capacity for understanding, that explanation and theory should be approached like adding seasoning to a meal, something that adds to and complements, without taking away the underlying flavor. For those interested in systemic constellation training, the authors' calendar, or contact information, see: www.ursula-franke.de or contact: tb@thomas-bryson.de.

Part One
Hospice

Death and Dying

Thomas Bryson and Dr. Ursula Franke-Bryson in Conversation

While I thought that I was learning how to live, I have been learning how to die.

Leonardo Da Vinci

Ursula: What is your personal interest in the subject of death?

Thomas: I didn't realize for much of my life that I was searching, or for what I was searching. It was only in hindsight that I found clarity. I had longed for a direct experience of life, unfiltered by the intellect. The risk-taking behaviors that I indulged in as a young man, were motivated by a desire for a sense of aliveness. Through good fortune and the guidance of wiser people than myself, I gained the insight that I could get the same sense of aliveness by simply taking emotional risks, without having the self-destructive side-effects of physical risk-taking. With that insight, I began to explore my fears, including the fear of death. I knew that by approaching death, I would be approaching life, and that the two cannot be separated.

After learning to see systemic patterns, I began to recognize that part of the story was that I had been unconsciously drawn to death my whole life, perhaps as a result of my father's unresolved wartime experiences. And looking further back in my lineage, I saw that my system had not completed the integration of events much more distant in time, things that only surfaced when my tools for self-inquiry improved.

U: How did you get involved in working with death and dying?

T: One evening in Portland, Oregon, I heard the former Harvard psychology professor Ram Dass, speaking about a time when he was in Varanassi, India, and had personally experienced people dying on the streets and had confronted his own death for the first time. Ram Dass, and what he had to say, resonated deeply with me. I craved that sense of aliveness, of freedom from seeing the world strictly through the lens of the need for personal survival. Looking back, I can see how mind, body and spirit were all parts of the journey. But at that time, I didn't perceive of it as a spiritual or psychological search, I just followed my inner sense of which direction to follow. The idea once came to me to become a hospice volunteer, even though at the time I didn't really know what that meant. So I went through the community hospice training and became a volunteer. Then one day, I realized that I wanted to go to nursing school, even though I didn't really know what that meant, either! Four years later, after leaving my profession as a graphic artist, I went to work as a nurse.

I had the idea that I should have some hospital experience after nursing school before I went into hospice. It was awful to work in the Veteran's Administration elder care ward in Portland. It seemed that it was more important to fill out the little boxes on the paperwork than it was to make sure that the patients were treated for their pain. What an eye opener! I would cry from stress nearly every night on the way home after work. I realized that I would have to quit, thinking, If this is what nursing is like, then I made a big mistake. But then, I got my first hospice job and it felt like I had come home. That is when I started my real education.

I have retired from nursing and now devote myself to systemic constellation therapy and training, I focus less on the actual process of dying, and instead look more into the inner structures that have been formed by our biographic and systemic encounters with death. I still try to be a catalyst in helping people to let go of their suffering through changing their relationship with both their inner and outer worlds.

U: Could you tell me more about hospice care?

T: In 2007, when I emigrated to Germany from the US, health care in America was rather dysfunctional. It was only when someone had a doctor who said that one had six months or less to live, were they guaranteed health care! Hospice is physical, emotional and spiritual care that is offered to a person and their family when a person is terminally ill and has chosen to seek comfort care, instead of actively seeking a cure. The focus of hospice is healing into life and death, not curing disease. As a hospice nurse, I worked in a team to provide that end of life care, initially in a special hospice nursing facility and then later, I traveled to wherever people were living and dying. Hospice nursing was both difficult and rewarding.

U: How is working in hospice different than working in a hospital?

T: Hospice nursing care is not restricted to a specific location, such as a hospital or care facility. Many of my patients were living and dying in their own homes. The hospice nurses had far greater autonomy to make decisions within guidelines, than hospital nurses. The philosophy of nursing which I followed, was to try to treat the patient's relationship to their disease. Medicine is concerned more with treating the disease itself. In hospice nursing, death was seen as something natural, rather than a problem that had to be surmounted. The patients were seen as individuals with emotional, physical and spiritual needs, not simply as diagnoses which were to be considered from the lofty intellectual distance of the medical model.

U: How was it for you to work in hospice?

T: It is impossible to describe the experience of intimately witnessing someone's last breath, or feeling a dying woman's pulse slowing to a stop under my fingers. Hospice was authentic. It was stepping into the reality which I had always craved, that had always been right there, but which I had somehow felt blocked from experiencing. The dying and their families taught me so much. It was difficult and emotionally challenging. And often intense, particularly when getting emergency calls from family members at all hours of the night, driving out to people's homes in the middle of nowhere and facing all the eccentricities of people who were under stress caring for their dying loved ones. It could be a challenge to address the nursing issues, while also being available to myself and taking the time to feel my own feelings. It can be hard to feel the emotions that come with the death of loved ones or those we feel empathy with; to stand by and not be able to do anything other than be present. It is easy to forget how important it is to simply be there, and how doing arises from being.

U: What do you think was blocking you from experiencing reality, as you put it?

T: Looking back, I see that I had not learned how to be present, nor understood the value of it. I was living most of the time in mental or emotional trances where I wasn't actually living in reality. Like everyone else, I have trauma in my ancestral lineage. I can say that it is obvious in hindsight, now that I have the eyes to see it and the resources to engage it and heal. I inherited systemic, trauma-response patterns, which were unconsciously affecting my behavior. Because of the intensity of the traumatic events and the lack of resources to stay present in the situations, I learned that it was better for me to look away, or to dissociate in the face of a reality which was too overwhelming for the people at the time of the trauma.

U: I know what you are speaking about. It sounds familiar to me from my own life story. What do you mean when you use the term 'trance'?

T: When I say trance, I mean a state of mind where the attention is unconsciously not directed towards the actual, real surroundings that can be perceived through the senses, like the person in front of you, his smile, haircut and look, or the sounds from the street and smell of the Spring morning. Instead the attention is directed to thoughts, images or emotions which arise from previous experiences, like sadness from a loss, or judgment that arise when one notices someone breaking social conventions.

But in this life now, living out a repeated pattern from the past, or mistaking the virtual reality of the mind for actual reality, doesn't serve my personal desire or the systemic movement toward a primary interchange with people and life. Only through that primary connection to life does new information enter the system. Seen from this perspective, my awakening serves the needs of the individual and of the lineage, as well as consciousness itself.

U: What kind of systemic trauma are you referring to?

T: War, untimely death, murder, genocide and rape - the usual suspects! In the course of working with death, dying and systemic trauma, a dark sense of humor surfaces. But seriously, these horrors are a widespread reality. We humans are part of a very aggressive species and have become our own worst enemies.

U: What do you think that you have learned from working with death and dying?

T: It impacted me on every level. I became grounded in reality and empowered there. I learned that when I don't resist heartbreak, that it can be a doorway to indescribable, poignant beauty and strength. Through exposure to death, concurrently with Zen meditation, I gained a depth of engagement with life that in some ways makes me ill-suited to ordinary relationships with people who avoid their inner worlds.

The reality of death is both much more mundane and more incredible than what I had thought. Several family members, who had taken care of their dying loved ones, said to me afterwards, *People who haven't experienced this, just don't understand. It was the most difficult, and at the same time, the most beautiful thing that I have ever experienced. I'd like to go on to become a hospice volunteer and do this to help others.*

Working with hospice and being exposed to non-traumatic death, I began to get my first glimpses of what it means to be human and to be an adult and stand alone in the face of death. I learned first-hand the difference between pain and suffering. I came to realize how beautiful and multi-dimensional people are, and to see how the specter of death separates the important things in life from the chaff. What matters most to people who are dying, is not how much money they have made or how successful they have been,

"War, untimely death, murder, genocide and rape – the usual suspects!"

but whether they have loved and have been loved. Nobody lies on their death bed and thinks, *I should have worked more.* It was reassuring to experience people dying peacefully, some even joyfully.

There is nothing wrong with death, we often just don't like the idea of it. But, dying is a natural process and our bodies know how to die. Like the way an antelope can go into a death state, moments before being pulled down by a cheetah, there are ways that the body has evolved to protect the psyche, as one becomes more distant and recedes from life.

On the professional level, hospice nursing was a laboratory exploring the essential human condition, where I learned to apply skills for dealing with difficult emotions that I use and teach regularly in my systemic practice. I started to understand fear, pain and human suffering through seeing and feeling what happens when people's personality structures loosen and come apart, when the normal coping strategies of knowing and being in control are no longer helpful.

U: After experiencing people coming to, and then going through the doorway what stays with you regarding death?

T: Like everything, death is not what we think it is. According to the *Tibetan Book of Living and Dying*, dying is a process which extends beyond what is called death in the west. In my own experience, I sometimes had a special connection, a resonance between myself and another person that persisted

for some time after the death of the person's body. I describe one of those occasions in the last of the *Stories from the Dying*.

Thinking, and hence cerebral knowing, is a reflection of reality that is always highly filtered. On another level, I would say that I can only truly know something by occupying the space of it, by being that something and seeing it from the inside, so to speak. Therefore, I don't personally know what it is like to be dead, and my many years of hospice experience have not filled that lack of knowing.

One's relationship with death says a lot about one's relationship to life. People often die the way they live. If a person is aggressive and uncaring, this might well result in a difficult, painful process of dying and can leave a legacy of suffering in their family when they die. If one knows how to accommodate to reality, one can be free of suffering at the time of death and leave behind a legacy of love and dignity. If one has unfinished emotional accounts waiting to be paid, one can stay in a dying body for a long time before all the emotional bills are resolved and one can let go. If one is stubborn, that can be excruciating. On the other hand, an insight gained in one moment can change a longstanding life pattern of fear into one of wonder and joy, even excitement, as is described in the first of the Stories from the Dying. When one is up to date with feeling one's emotions, crossing the boundary between life and death can be as simple as exhaling, without the need to take another inhale. Often, the moment of death looks like a very gentle releasing, subtler than slipping out of a tight shoe. The worry lines between the eyebrows relax, the face loses its normal tension and sometimes there is the most beautiful little smile playing about the lips. I remember one woman who had been unresponsive for a week, just lying in her bed. One moment, she just sat up in bed with the most indescribable expression of joyful surprise on her face - and died.

U: Why then, do you think that people are afraid of death?

T: People are afraid to die because death seems like the end of one's identity, of one's personal world. It is natural to have fear of pain and of dying, but it seems that the fear of loss of control and of losing one's self-concept is a central element in suffering.

Humans evolved as potential prey within a food-chain. Our physical, psychological, emotional and behavioral instincts reflect that. Fear for one's self, group and offspring, is part of an instinctive response pattern which is designed for self-preservation.

U: You said that you learned that there was a difference between pain and suffering. Could you elaborate on that?

T: One of my main functions in hospice nursing was to treat pain. Pain is a signal to the brain that something is out of balance. Physical pain comes when the body is being damaged. It is personal and subjective, and can be made worse through resistance and tension. Pain comes to everyone at some time in their lives. Emotional or spiritual pain is also an indication that something is subjectively wrong, but instead of being restricted to the personal level, it can also be on the interpersonal or transpersonal levels.

In contrast, suffering is resistance to what is. I have heard the Zen master Adyashanti say, Have you ever noticed that when you resist reality, that you lose? Suffering is that resistance, that wanting reality to be different, either wanting something one doesn't have, or not wanting something that one does have. Suffering comes with every identity, but it is optional, if one learns how to say yes to life and reality - and not to take one's identity too seriously.

U: How is identity related to suffering?

T: Identity is hardwired with angst and resistance to death. The person whom one assumes oneself to be, dies.

Identity functions as a key part of the human survival instinct; to organize experience and evaluate it on the basis of its utility for the survival of the individual, the group and the genetic lineage. Like the security software on your computer, part of the function of the human survival mechanism is to defend the survival mechanism itself. All threats to the identity, including death, trigger resistance and instinctual, self-protective coping strategies.

In evolutionary terms, the self-concept was the basis for conceptual thinking and identity. The development of conceptual thinking was probably the key innovation in mental software responsible for The Great Leap Forward, when Homo sapiens became more successful than other pre-historic hominids, and came eventually to dominate the planet. While short-term survival served the rise of H. sapiens, it has become biologically insupportable. Long ago, the greatest short-term danger to humans ceased to be animal predators and became other humans. My father always pointed out that tshere are simply too many humans on the planet and we will have larger and larger die-offs of the population as it comes into balance.

U: Do you think that people need to finish their emotional tasks in order to die easily?

T: Yes, on the level of personal identity, but the question begs for a more complete context which includes the systemic and transpersonal levels.

On the personal level, having unresolved, unintegrated emotional material can interfere with both living fully and dying easily. As death approaches, time is more recognizably limited. As one is caught in the dying process, there may not be enough resources or time to resolve outstanding items. When death comes unexpectedly or quickly, the chance for personally resolving things is suddenly over. The option for doing what needs to be done in your life is gone.

The delicate point, is that your personal unresolved emotional tasks, include all the unresolved emotional tasks which have been handed down to you through the generations.

U: This is what is reflected in Fairy Tales like The Flying Dutchman or The Ancient Mariner who still have to be redeemed somehow before they can find peace and die.

T: Or the Hungry Ghosts in some Buddhist traditions - people with a huge appetite but mouths so small that they can't ever fill their inner emptiness.

On the systemic level, it seems that some representatives in constellations are like Hungry Ghosts. They represent people who need something, but don't know that they are dead, and so can't find either redemption or peace through letting go into death. These people are the ones who through untimely death or trauma leave legacies that show up later as symptoms in our clients. In the systemic view, unintegrated and resolved inheritances relating to war, genocide, violent or untimely death, are what some call the karma of one's lineage.

On the transpersonal level, spiritual seekers can be in a similar repetitive pattern of searching for fulfillment in their lives. Without having developed the inner personal structure which allows them to be able to receive what is offered by reality, their search can never be fulfilled. The tenacity of holding on to their identities does not allow the seekers to relax into who they actually, already are.

Many people who have had authentic tastes of the underlying reality, the Unborn, as the great Zen master Bonki called it, are repeatedly pulled back into self-defense postures, when there is too much unresolved personal and systemic emotional material. That was my own experience, until there were both enough inner resources to resolve the arising karmic debts and enough clarity through repeated dipping into the well of silence, to completely see through the identity.

It can be confusing that three apparently different things are true at the same time. We are unique individuals who die, we are literally the extension of the lives of our ancestors, and at the same time, we are the timeless presence which was never born and does not die.

U: Could you speak about how spirituality has been relevant to your work with death?

T: In my work caring for the dying and their families as a hospice nurse, I was required by law to provide spiritual care, as well as physical and emotional care. My patient population was relatively diverse for the USA, but it was not so diverse when compared to the immense range in belief and practice relating to death and to grief in cultures around the world.

In my practice, I had to adapt my spiritual language to that of my patients and their families, and yet in order to have any credibility, I had to remain congruent with my own perspective. I learned to speak about the core of spirituality in a relatively culture-neutral way, so that I could have and maintain better rapport with people with differing belief systems.

The religions that I am familiar with, which are a small fraction of the world's religions, all have something to say about death, what comes afterwards, and how one should behave while living. From my own background in Zen, and my love of the view from the mountain, so to speak, I find it interesting that they speak of something in addition to, something beyond the cycle of life and death; for instance, in the ideas of Everlasting Life in Christianity, Escape from the Wheel of Samsara in Hinduism, a return to the Great Father in some native traditions, or in the recognition of our Unborn nature in Zen Buddhism. I think that all the stories are true from their own perspectives, but I can only speak with any expertise when it comes to my own experience, and that is subject to interpretation!

But, in my hospice experience, religious belief systems and concepts didn't seem to be enough at the time of death. Death is extremely grounded in reality, so I found practical

Lycaon pictus Grant Reed Letaka Safaris

spirituality to be much more useful than theoretical spirituality. Some of the worst deaths I was ever aware of, were those by devout believers. The modern Christian message seemed to be, It's going to be beautiful when you get to heaven.'What that really meant, was that while the future will be better, the present moment was left unresolved. It said, Here and now it is not okay. The solace of Christ and God are marooned somewhere in the future and not available in this moment of suffering.

U: When you say 'practical spirituality,' what do you mean?

T: When I was working as a nurse with the families of dying people, I noticed that the family members tended to suffer, sometimes far more, than the actual person whose death was becoming a closer reality. The families were often faced with many intense, unknown and unexplored emotions without adequate resources to feel them. It was sometimes their first ever encounter with such strong emotions. The quantity and quality of the emotions which were suddenly there to be felt, were frequently overwhelming, keeping the person from being present for their dying loved one or with their own direct experiences.

As a way to help reduce their suffering, I began to apply what I had learned in my Aikido and Zen practices. I had learned that it is more empowering to go directly to the emotion itself and feel it, rather than coping with the emotions by keeping a distance and to think the feelings instead of feeling them. This simplicity is counter-intuitive for many people. It is perfectly natural and customary that one searches for information and control when facing difficult situations, and that one would avoid unpleasant emotions or not have the resources to enter into these sometimes dark places.

I remember one woman whose mother was dying. She really wanted to spend her mother's last moments or hours with her, but she was so overwhelmed by her own fear of death and the thoughts about the suffering that her mother might be facing, that she couldn't stay in the room with her. When I demonstrated to her that when she felt her emotions as sensations, instead of as thoughts, she was empowered, it completely changed her experience. She smiled and was able to spend the rest of the day with her mother in great intimacy before she died.

U: How did you learn about the power of presence?

T: The power of presence is so simple that it eludes most people, even though it is easy to demonstrate. The Witness is something that is hiding in plain sight as my father used to say. It is simply what is looking out one's eyes. I call this presence, because it is usually an easy concept to which one can relate.

There was a sequence of events which brought me to this recognition. It started with a deep experience of my mind being utterly silenced while on a spiritual retreat in the Cascade Mountains of Oregon. To my great surprise, I found two days later, that the silent presence that I had found, was directly applicable to the martial art of Aikido. Then, in my nursing practice, I started using it as something which I thought of as Emotional Aikido. From there, I brought the concept and practice into Systemic Constellation.

I experienced the witness one night when I was on retreat in the mountains in Oregon. I had watched a dancer by the name of Zuleikha performing the Mevlana whirling dance that originated with the Sufi master Jalal al-Din Rumi. I was completely mesmerized, thinking that the dance was only possible because God was dancing her, and by extension, that God was dancing all of us. When the dance ended, I had no will to move. My mind was silenced. I walked like a drunk through the starlight to my favorite thermal pool in the far meadow and sat in the warm water for some hours. In the stillness, the night sky was simply above and the reflected stars were below. In between the stars and their reflection on the water, there was only silent witnessing. Occasionally in those hours, I would notice that in my mind's eye, there seemed to be a multi-colored, moving ball, like a crumpled piece of colorful foil, visible in the lower left quadrant of my inner eye. This object seemed to rise in an arc across my inner view until it was top center, and then it would reveal its contents to me. This object within my perception was carrying a thought! After the thought was displayed, like a subtitle in a foreign film, it disappeared.

The actual power of this witnessing perspective became apparent to me after the retreat, when I went back to where I was practicing the traditional Japanese martial art of Aikido. That evening, we students were faced with a difficult test. We were to sit on our knees on the tatami mat, bow our foreheads to the mat, and then to stand up from our knees while being prevented from rising by two others, who were standing and holding us down. If we did our meditation correctly, we would not be disturbed or perceive the two holding us as obstacles. However, I was not following the rules and meditating the way that I was supposed to. I was simply resting in the place of the witness. Without effort, I did the exercise and the two holding me flew off! I still remember the big smile on the face of the Sensei.

Agama agama

In that moment, I realized that this vantage point, when one stays in the body, is the heart of Aikido and what is called Beginner's Mind in Zen. It is the power of embodied presence. Spiritual seekers with whom I was familiar up until that time, normally avoided talking about their own power. They seemed more interested in seeking some sort of transcendent purity. In fact, feeling one's feelings in the body and staying present is a tremendous resource for facing the inheritance of one's birth. To walk through this life with dignity and grace as embodied presence, personal power is helpful. One can never actually get away from the difficult emotions that come with incarnation within a lineage. The question remains, how to feel and deal with them?

It is easy to teach and to grasp and experience the concept and practice of being empowered by staying present and in one's body. We teach it regularly in systemic constellation training and in private practice.

U: What do you see as the relevance of exploring death for systemic constellation?

T: I see three aspects really. The first is that systemic constellation is an effective tool for assisting in the organization of one's emotional affairs and finishing large pieces of unfinished emotional business, making it much easier to have a peaceful death. It can be used with dying patients or family members, or with people whose death is less imminent.

The second aspect, is that our survival instincts and all the mental, emotional, behavioral and psychological structures that go with them, are the fundamental features of the psychological complexes that face clients who come to therapy. Through the resource of presence, one can more readily develop a better relationship with death, and an understanding of the mechanisms humans have evolved in order to avoid death and the thoughts and emotions related to it. Having this resource and knowledge personally, we as therapists are better equipped to help our clients to live a more peaceful life with more freedom of choice, rather than lives guided by out-dated programming.

The last aspect, is that while our inherited library of experiences is biased towards topics that relate to avoiding death, that is not the whole story. Traumas, rapes, murders, genocides and wars leave a red thread through a lineage. They are the experiences that leave a legacy of tension, fear and suffering.

But, these are just the responses which show up in the foreground. We also have a long, rich heritage of peaceful, natural deaths. We have many ancestors who have lived full lives, were engaged in life, were present for each other and who died easily when it was time. That deep heritage is also accessible in the moment that we stop listening to our internal Disaster Committee, endlessly arguing over what is the worst possible thing that could happen. It is equally possible to come into our own actual experience now, and to make contact with our breath, bodies and environment.

One can imagine what it would feel like after we are already dead. After we have died, nothing can hurt us anymore and there is no need to be afraid. There is no longer any danger in not belonging. We can be willing to let go of the child's need to belong and to let our identity serve our undying self, instead of demanding that we serve it, then life changes.

A moment in the presence of the Beloved and the course of the river changes.

Miracle of Love, Stories about Neem Karoli Baba

Stories from the Dying

Lycaon pictus and *Acacia*

When one asks, What is death like?, there are no reliable answers. The following section is made up of stories from the dying, just eleven out of many, which stood out in my years of hospice nursing and volunteering. Taken together, they are like a good question - they open a space which one can step into, but they don't give answers. The first is a story of a woman who drew back the curtain and took a look at what was on the other side of the veil.

It will be exciting!

Susan was an attractive, dark haired woman in her mid-forties. Because of her disease progression, she had been unable to get out of her bed for over a month. She spent hours looking at her hand held mirror, grooming her hair, perfecting her facial make-up and taking care of her fingernails. If one was unaware of the disease process hidden underneath the bedcovers, she looked perfect. But her brittleness was apparent.

Susan was terrified. She was unable to voice the words hospice, cancer or death. She had a very frightened girlfriend who would visit regularly. And she had a fundamentalist Christian preacher who would come to visit her in her room at the hospice facility. He was what is called a 'fire and brimstone' preacher, talking about sin and damnation, essentially using the fear of hell as a motivation for people to believe and behave in the proper way.

One morning, Susan's nurse Colleen, seemed to be listening to an inner voice. She turned to me in the medication room where we were working and said, *I think Susan needs me!* She went down to the patient's room. Lying in her bed, Susan looked like she was dead. Usually, dead people are immediately recognizable as being dead, as if there is just some inner knowing which recognizes death. But suddenly, Susan gasped, and took in a large, noisy gulp of air. She looked at Colleen and said, *Oh, there you are, I was just down the hall looking for you. She smiled. I wanted to tell you, that I just took a test flight!*

The two talked about it and it seemed that Susan had been traveling about without using her body. We didn't really know what her actual experience was, but she smiled more and seemed much more relaxed, less brittle. That afternoon, her terrified girlfriend came to visit her after work again, as usual. Susan smiled and proceeded to tell her friend, *I took a test-flight this morning.* Her friend stopped breathing and looked at her with eyes wide. Susan put a hand on her friend's arm and said gently, *Oh, don't be afraid. It will be exciting!* Later she called her preacher and told him not to come anymore, saying, *I don't need you anymore.* She lived completely peacefully for another month, and then one morning, she just didn't wake up again.

Commentary

There was a noticeable difference in Susan after she had what was apparently an out-of body experience, her test flight - she was no longer suffering. Something she had seen or experienced had told her that death wasn't what she thought it would be, in fact was something to look forward to with excitement. Her fear was gone. Instead of being a disempowered person, clutching the hand of her equally disempowered friend, she reassured her friend. Something had happened, which meant that she no longer needed the worldview of fear and control that had been her belief system up until then.

Nephila inaurata

Eight Hours with the Dead

A woman in her eighties died at seven in the morning, in a small in-patient hospice nursing facility, just at the time when the day staff took over from the night shift. It was common for people to die when there was a change of energy, either when the shift changed or when a visitor came or had left.

The dead woman's adult daughter had been with her through the night and was now sitting by the bedside where her mother's body lay. As her mother was on her journey from illness, to diagnosis, to death, the daughter was on her own journey of growth through facing this time as well as she could. As part of that journey, she had absorbed some of the traditional Tibetan Buddhist teachings that Sogyal Rinpoche had written about in The Tibetan Book of Living and Dying. In the high desert plateau of Tibet, it was the tradition that the body of the newly dead not be moved for a period of forty days. In that time, the deceased would be read to in order to be guided through the different realms encountered after death. It was intended to help the deceased to either recognize fully their true nature, and to know that everything which was experienced was a creation of their mind, or at least to be steered to a favorable rebirth, so that the journey of their soul could continue well.

After her mother had died, the daughter asked if she could leave the body where it was and that we not have it moved. I agreed. In the state of Oregon, where I was working, I could leave the woman's body where it was for up to 24 hours without getting undue notice from the regulatory authorities. I occasionally checked on the daughter who continued to sit quietly with her mother's corpse throughout the day. As I was finishing my shift in the afternoon, I heard laughter coming from the room. I went in and asked, *What is so funny?*

The daughter said, *As you know, I have been sitting here now, all day long. It is absolutely clear to me beyond a doubt, that this body is dead. It could be a lock of hair or a fingernail clipping just lying there. My mother used this body for a time, but now that is over. She has nothing more to do with that body lying there. What is funny, is that when I look into my heart, where I have my relationship with my mother, nothing has changed! I can talk to her just like I used to when she was alive, and in my mind I can hear all her answers, just as if she were sitting here with me. Take the body. It doesn't mean a thing!* She stood up, smiled, and walked out of the facility.

Commentary

It wouldn't be practical in America to leave a body where it had died for forty days. What seemed important to me was that the daughter renewed her connection with her mother in her inner world. She listened to her own inner voice and did what felt right to her, regardless of what was 'right' for anyone else.

How to behave and think about death and what happens after death is highly culturally defined. What passes for appropriate in one culture may be the exact opposite of what is done in another. Different cultures have a very wide range of approaches to behavior toward the body and to mourners after death (see Dancing on the Grave: Encounters with Death by Nigel Barley). Some cultures freely express their grief quite openly, are even expected to display their tears, while in other cultures grief is hidden away. Rituals of sitting with the body, cleaning it or dressing it in fine clothes, wailing or receiving neighbors to mourn together, are some of the many ways of honoring the body and the person who was dear. Cultural rituals allow time to accommodate to the reality of death and to allow one's emotions time to be felt at their own pace. The ancient Egyptians had extensive rituals to ensure that the dead had a good afterlife. In China, the dead and talking of them is avoided, as if it is contagious. In many cultures, humor plays a large part in the process of relating to death and the dead. In Ireland and Germany, celebrations with alcohol, music and dancing are ways to honor the dead, express one's feelings to others and to celebrate that life continues. The Mevlana Sufis celebrate the hour of death of the great mystic poet, Jalaluddin Rumi. His tomb in Konya, Turkey, continues to be a pilgrimage site which has a very special atmosphere.

*Wanderers,
worshipers,
lovers of
leaving,
come!*

**Jalal al-Din
Rumi**

Angel Band

Late one evening, I was called out to visit a dying woman and her family. She lived in a small, working class home in a mostly conservative town. In the living room was the patient lying in her hospital bed. Her two daughters and other family members were with her. From my physical assessment, I recognized that she was very near to death, but I had no idea when she would complete her task of dying. She was not fully conscious, her breath was shallow and irregular. Her lungs made a harsh raspy sound and her pulse was quite fast, at 140 beats per minute. I gave her a very small dose of liquid morphine to ease her breathing.

The two daughters were standing by their mother. The sisters, who had been professional singers, began to sing a beautiful, contemporary, upbeat gospel song, blending their similar voices in close harmony. The song was about how everyone in heaven was joyous that would join them. They sang about how Jesus was eagerly waiting to embrace her, now that she was on her way home. They sang of how the feast was all ready and everyone was waiting to celebrate with her. On impulse, I put my hand on her wrist, and felt her pulse as they sang. The heartbeat was now only 45! With the last notes of the song fading away, her pulse slowed to a stop. They had sang her across the threshold.

As we waited for the mortuary to send someone to pick up the body, I stood in the tiny kitchen with the two daughters. The older sister turned on a small television set which sat on top of the refrigerator. She said, *Once in awhile, it is just too much for me, to feel everything. Then sometimes, I need to zone out and watch television for a little while.*

Commentary

Music is strong medicine. In the year 1500, in early Spanish hospices, Christian, Jewish and Islamic patients were all prescribed musical treatment through the use of the same psalms, in addition to the pain medication which was available at the time. The psalms were sung to the patient by a special choir, using different musical modes, each with its own mood, depending on where the patient was in their dying process.

The peace and beauty of the experience listening to the sisters sing, while feeling their mother's pulse slip away under my fingertips, is not really describable. When the daughter intentionally went into a television trance, she was aware of what she was doing. Substituting a trance that is more easily controlled, such as through watching television, or changing states through taking a walk, or napping when things are overwhelming, can be a strategic retreat - a stepping out of one's state and moving towards regaining a place of greater choice.

A Lover of God

I was to make my first visit to a woman cancer patient staying in a nursing facility. She was in her mid seventies, and was expected to die in 24 to 36 hours, as she was no longer able to eat or drink and her bowels and kidneys had stopped functioning. It was reported that she was in severe pain, but was refusing to take any pain medication. I was challenged to help her find relief from her pain.

As I came to the door of her room and looked in, the woman looked up at me and our eyes met. There was a recognition of some sort that took place in that moment, as though we were both together in exactly the right place and time. I introduced myself and came to sit by her bedside. She talked extensively about what a good Christian she was and how she was assured of a place in heaven for her many good works. After ten or fifteen minutes of talking, she was exhausted and I took the chance to respond.

I said to her, *When you first saw me in the door, you knew that I was a lover of God, just like you.* She smiled, in recognition of her own perception.

But I must warn you. My spirituality is practical, not theoretical, because I am a nurse. Some of the words that I use may not be exactly what you are used to. I suggest that you listen with your heart, and if my words resonate there and find a home, then you will know that they are true.

She smiled and said, *Alright.*

I went on, *God is everywhere.* This was safe.

God comes to the trees in the form of water, sunlight and earth, just as they are needed.

She said, *I never thought about it that way!*

Since God is everywhere, that means that he is here with you in this room, too. When you lean back on the pillow on your bed, God is holding it for you.

She relaxed a little more, as a sign of consent.

And you have an eternal soul. She nodded.

Since your soul is eternal, it means that it must include this moment now.

She was paying close attention now, her face a little brighter.

That means that God and your eternal soul are right here, right now as we are speaking! She liked this.

And when you get to heaven (of course she knew she was going to heaven), *God is going to yell at you.*

She was crestfallen. In a little voice, she asked, *Why?*

He is going to say to you, I sent you a perfectly good hospice nurse with medication to take away your pain. Why have you turned away from me?

After I had gone, she asked the staff for the pain medication they had offered her earlier. She found that it worked very well for her. She died peacefully and pain free the next day. Afterwards, her husband was very happy about their last hours together, and the way that the *missionary hospice nurse* had helped his wife have such a beautiful passing into death.

Commentary

There is no way to objectively measure pain. It is a completely subjective experience, but it is normally tiring. Resisting pain takes away psychic and physical energy. Energy that could be well used for other things, such as relating to one's loved ones, or reviewing one's life and coming to completion with it in the time remaining. Some remarkable people are able to feel pain and not resist it. For others, pain holds special meaning for them. It seemed that this woman had some religious ideals about suffering that drove her to resist seeking relief for her pain, perhaps based on teachings about Christ's suffering at the time of his crucifixion.

We truly saw each other in that moment when our eyes met. There was immediate rapport between us. That allowed me to bring her faith in God and eternity into focus in this present moment. As I used language which was consistent with her beliefs, I could give her an easier, less Spartan interpretation of her pain. When her symptoms were well controlled, she had more available energy and was able to continue her process with ease and dignity. Her death became a journey in which her husband could be inspired and participate fully.

Buteo augur Ursula Franke

Dresden

All the man's children knew that their father was getting close to death and they had made the pilgrimage from all around the country to be at his bedside. At each visit, I would do an assessment of the patient and then would talk to the family, tell them what I was seeing and ask how they were doing. The man was no longer eating or drinking, did not speak, open his eyes or give any indication that he noticed other people. His skin was thin and almost transparent. His pulse, weak and irregular. His breathing would have episodes of being rapid and then stop for up to twenty seconds. He seemed ready to die at any time.

A family member responded: *Yes, but he has been like this for three weeks! What is keeping him alive, I wonder? We need to take care of business at home as well. How long do you think it will be?*

Sitting in the small apartment, I asked them about his life, where he had lived, what had happened in his life. They told me that he had grown up in Germany before he had emigrated to the United States. He and his family had lived in Dresden during the war. The city was a cultural center with many beautiful churches and other historical buildings. The city was full of refugees fleeing the destruction and starvation as the Second World War staggered to its end. Despite the fact that the city had no apparent military significance, the British and Americans had dropped the new phosphor fire bombs on the city. Nearly 100,000 civilians were burned to death in the ensuing firestorm. Most of his family had been killed, unable to escape the fire.

I went into his room and sat beside his bed. His face looked tense. His breathing was now fast and ragged. I said to him, *All your family is safe now. Your parents and grandparents have all come down to the river. The water is cool. Everyone is all right. Nothing can hurt anyone now. You don't need to worry about anyone anymore, they are just fine, now.* As I talked to him, his breathing slowed down and become smooth. His face lost its tension and seemed peaceful. That evening, while the children were all still there, the man slipped into death.

Commentary

Physiologically, the man appeared to be ready to die, but apparently there was something keeping him alive. All his children being there with him was not enough, so I looked for more information from the family. I intuited that the trauma of the firebombing of Dresden and the death of so many, including his relatives, must have had a strong impact on him as a young boy. I used a guided visualization, painting a simple soothing picture with a new ending to that long ago trauma. His body relaxed as I spoke with him and he was finally able to give in to death.

Marathon

Jim was in his early fifties. Like many long distance runners, he was tall and lanky. He had been a high level athlete and coach. He said that his athletic success was partly because he had learned how to overcome the pain in his body when he was running. He could push himself to excel in his races, often to the point of vomiting and collapse after the race was over. While these skills served him in his athletic career, it made his dying process personally difficult.

His dying process was a marathon. The drawn out nature of his dying and suffering were challenging to the hospice staff, who had concepts about what constituted a good death. Younger, healthier people often take more time to die of cancer than do older people, as it takes longer for the disease to physically overwhelm them. Jim had an array of tubes running into and out of his body. When he would take a drink of orange juice, a moment later, orange liquid would run out of a tube coming out of the side of his body. When his bladder worked, another tube lead the urine into a bag. His bowels were likewise diverted out of his gut into a pouch. He had pain medication going through a tube directly into his spine, as well as another one going into a vein. And when he was short of breath, he could get oxygen from a tube in his nose. When Jim would be reclining in his bed with his mouth hanging open, his eyes rolled back in his head and his skin ashen, the nurses would wonder if he had passed through death's door. But then, he would perk up at bit and continue with living. One weekend, he organized all of his tubes and drove himself to the coast alone to go bird watching.

For years there had been bitter, sharp, divisions and conflicts that had separated Jim and all of his brothers, one from each other. When Jim was finally too weak to leave his room, his brothers and their wives all came together in the same place for the very first time. They started talking and discussing things, approaching each other while having to spend time together. At the end of an intense month of repeated episodes of excruciating pain, Jim finally was no longer successfully resisting death and died. Ironically, the result of his marathon was that it gave Jim and his brothers the time and emotional pressure they needed to heal their differences and come to a place of profound peace together.

Commentary

On one level, Jim's marathon seemed to be a continuation of a long pattern of exerting will power over feeling physical or emotional pain. But on another level, his perseverance in the face of pain, was exactly what was needed - it allowed him and his family to find profound healing. In my own interpretation, it felt Christ-like in the way that Jim took on this final dying marathon and in the process of extending his own suffering, gave the gift of peace to a family that was in such need of it.

The Ritual

Richard was quite open and relaxed about coming to the hospice facility to die. He only had two requests: He wanted to watch his favorite basketball team on television, and he wanted to smoke cigars. But within just a few days, he had very quickly declined to the point where he was too weak to smoke and the basketball season was still some months away. He had a group of pleasant, rather matter-of-fact friends, who were looking after him and keeping him company. They reported that he had always been a peaceful, organized person and that he had no incomplete business to take care of or people he needed to see. One afternoon, Richard was lying unconscious on his back in his bed with his hands neatly folded on his chest. His friends were all there with him.

One of them said to me, We all think that Richard is ready to die. *You are his nurse. Don't you have a ritual or something that you do?*

I took a mental step backwards and thought for a moment, and then said, *What I do, is that I listen to my heart, and then I do what it tells me.*

The man asking looked a bit puzzled and said, *Like what?*

Following my own advice, I looked inward and felt my way into the situation. I sat next to Richard's bed, placed a hand on his hands, and said to him, *Richard, all your friends are here. Everything is taken care of. They will be alright. If you are ready to go, it would be fine if you were to die.* Within five minutes, Richard took his last breath. With the help of the friends, the staff cleaned his body and dressed him in a shirt from his favorite sports team. We put one of his cigars between his fingers and sent his body off to the mortuary.

Commentary

Spontaneous rituals can be very simple, yet effective, while more traditional rituals can sometimes lose their spark. It is said that hearing is the last of the senses to leave one as the doors of death open. It appeared that all Richard needed was to be told that everything was alright so that he could go.

Quieting the Demons

He was a very muscular military veteran who had served in the Vietnam War, what the Vietnamese call the American War. He seemed to have some internal demons. He repeatedly relived his wartime experiences through watching war movies. He was a tense, willful authoritarian, who was very much the head of the household. He had a history of drugs, alcohol and violence, before he stopped drinking and had a conversion to fundamental Christianity. He had married a Vietnamese woman whom he had met through his church. Together they had a son and daughter. As his disease took his strength and control away from him, the patient had high levels of anxiety. Although he was too weak to stand, he was repeatedly getting up out of bed and then falling, saying, *I have to do something*, although he didn't know what it was that he kept trying to accomplish.

Because of his history of drug and alcohol use, he had a very high tolerance for the kind of medication that he was taking to try to control his anxiety. Instead of taking away his anxiety, it simply took away his consciousness. When the medication wore off and he woke up, he struggled just as hard as he had before the medication had put him to sleep.

It was difficult for his wife to ask for or to receive help. As her husband neared the end of his life, she was completely exhausted by the ordeal of taking care of him. The two college age children came to spend the night and take care of him, so that she could get her first night's sleep in quite some time. I made a late-night - early morning visit in response to the son calling for help with his father. The father was in a highly agitated state when I arrived. The son and daughter had been sitting on either side of his bed, trying to calm him down. They were quite stressed that all the medication just wasn't working. When they got talking, they confided to me that they were both uncomfortable with their parents rigid religion and they were both actually practicing Buddhists. They very much wanted to take away his years of suffering, which seemed to be coming to a peak now. I taught them an active meditation which they could use which I had been taught by Roshi Joan Halifax at the Upaya Zen Center. The Tonglen meditation, as it is called, originates from before the beginning of Tibetan Buddhism. It is a breathing meditation intended to transform suffering. One is mindful and focuses on the in-breath. One imagines that one is inhaling all of the suffering of the other person, as if one is inhaling thick, black smoke. One imagines that the smoke enters the heart, one feels the pain of the other and the heart cracks open. When the heart opens, it releases light. On the exhale, one imagines this light streaming out, giving peace and comfort to the one who is suffering.

I came back several hours later when the father had died. The son and daughter had been sitting next to their father doing the Tonglen meditation. As they breathed in his suffering and breathed out peace, their father calmed down, until all three of them fell asleep. In the darkest hour before dawn, his breathing changed and the two woke up. They reached out, each holding one of his hands as he died. As we waited for the body to be taken to the mortuary, the son told me that he was planning on going to nursing school in a year when he finished his undergraduate college. I was proud of them. I told him, *You and your sister are already doing master level nursing.*

Commentary

For some patients with deep seated anxiety, the pharmaceutical solution is ineffective. And I felt that the rigid thinking and diminished level of awareness of this man, meant that there was no opening through which I could work directly with him cognitively. The son and daughter were willing to try my suggestion and were empowered by using an old pre-Buddhist tradition which felt deeper to them than the new Christianity of their parents.

Brenda's Vision

Brenda was only forty five years old. She had had a short, intense life as a drug addict. Theoretically, she was staying in the in-patient hospice facility to die of HIV disease, but she still had things to do. When she received her monthly disability check, she would take a taxi downtown and go on a binge for a few days, then call the hospice and ask if someone could pick her up. Once the staff was cleaning her room while Brenda was out on the town and discovered that she had only been pretending to take the incredibly expensive medications that the hospice was providing for her in order to reduce the symptoms of her disease. Instead, of taking them, she threw them into her dresser drawer. The administrator of the facility asked her to find another place to stay saying, *This room can be used by someone who is more serious about what we have to offer. When it comes to the time when you are ready to come back, you will always be welcome here.*

Brenda's return appearance in the hospice was in style. One afternoon, I heard loud laughter. It was Brenda being pushed up the hall in a wheelchair towards the nurses' station. The skin of her emaciated body was stretched tight over her skull which was partially shrouded by the black hood of her sweatshirt and she carried a cane in her hand like the scepter of death.

She had stopped taking drugs and had made a traditional conversion to Christianity. Her room was now adorned with crucifixes on every wall and available surface. As she weakened and was no longer able to get out of bed, her world got smaller. But the whole side of her room was a large window looking out into a beautiful forest. From her room, one could see only nature, with no sign that man had ever set foot there.

One day in her room, I was feeding Brenda her favorite food, strips of toasted white bread dipped in hot cocoa. As she looked out of her window, she exclaimed, *Look at that! Look at that!*

I bent over to be at her eye level as I looked out into the forest. There amongst the trees, some twenty meters away, perfectly obvious, were three white crosses. The cross in the center was somewhat larger and set forward from the other two, as in traditional Christian iconography. As I watched, the crosses faded and became like a mirage and disappeared.

Brenda went into ecstasy! Tears of joy streamed down her face. Her face became positively angelic as she repeated over and over, *This is so sweet. This is so sweet.* As she started to drift back into her normal way of being, I caught her eyes and we just gazed at each other and she would light up again. Brenda had always been a difficult patient. She was highly manipulative and demanding that everything be minutely organized to her satisfaction. But now, she was completely full of love for everything in the world and everyone in it. Staff members who had avoided coming into her room became drawn in just to be with the presence that was shining through her being. Her mother stayed with her for the next 48 hours while Brenda was in her state of ecstasy. Later she said, *My daughter was more alive in those last two days than she had been in her entire life put together.* After those two days, Brenda lost consciousness, but continued to live for nearly a week. When the body finally dropped away, it was so completely used up that the skin was literally starting to fall off her bones.

Commentary

I was fortunate enough to have shared a vision that Brenda was having. In that vision, she got exactly what she needed in precisely the imagery that she cherished. There was so much left unresolved in her short life, that only something greater could resolve it all so that she could find peace.

Often as a therapist, one enters partially into the trance field of the client, perceiving it as if from the inside. There are a number of models which attempt to explain the occurrence, but still cannot settle it. The therapist may perceive images, sensations or other perceptions that are sourced in the client.
Old Flames

Old Flames

I went to visit Elizabeth in her home once each week for six months. I always looked forward to seeing her. She was an intelligent and articulate woman in her early sixties. The nursing visits often took place in the garden and did not include more physical assessment than my asking, How are you today? Usually, we would talk about things that interested us both, like birds or archeology and I would always bring my mandolin and play her some old time fiddle music. She favored the bluesy sounds of Bill Monroe.

She had a terminal cancer diagnosis, but had chosen not to have it treated. Instead, she had decided to take advantage of Oregon's law which allowed physician's assisted suicide if the patient met certain criteria. Elizabeth met those. She said that she would know when it was time to go when her quality of life declined to a point which she found unacceptable. I respected her right to choose her own path. She intended to die alone, but as the time grew closer, she gave in to her friends' wishes to be able to be with her when she died.

Elizabeth was a private person with a lot of dignity. She knew that it was important for her friends to be there when she died, but she didn't want to be a spectacle, saying, *I don't want a bunch of vultures sitting around, staring at me as I die.* She requested that I come and play my mandolin as she died, so that her friends would be distracted.

On her chosen afternoon, her friends assembled and I entertained the group with a number of old tunes on the mandolin. Two people from the organization, Death with Dignity, came by her house to help with the procedure. Elizabeth had filled her order at the pharmacy, for one hundred times the lethal dose of barbiturates. One woman from the organization emptied the capsules into a small glass and made a slurry with some apple juice, while the other acted as a witness. An hour before Elizabeth was planning on drinking it, she had taken some anti-nausea medication, so that there would be less chance of vomiting the deadly cocktail.

In accordance with the ethics guidelines of the hospice organization for which I worked, I stepped out of the house when Elizabeth took the lethal dose of prescribed barbiturate. After she had finished drinking, I came back into the living room where she and her friends were. Elizabeth was lying on her couch, her head on the lap of a close friend. I picked up my mandolin and played while singing her an old, sweet love song, called, *Old flames can't hold a candle to you.* I was quite surprised that I had enough breath control to get through the song.

The last verse and chorus went,

Sometimes at night, I think of old lovers I've known.
How holding them close to me, made me not feel so alone.
Then I feel you beside me and even those memories are gone,
like the stars in the night, after the first light of dawn.

Old flames can't hold a candle to you.
No one can light up my life like you do.
Flickering embers of love, I've known one or two,
but old flames, can't hold a candle to you.

As I was finishing the chorus, she took off her glasses, looked me in the eyes, and with a sweet smile, went into a swoon. In a few minutes her breathing stopped.

I could see that the friends were stunned. I managed to be professional and offered a healing ritual for the group. I was shaken and unable to work the rest of the day. For some years, I was unable to sing the song without tears. Now, they still come easily.

Commentary

The way people live and die affects those around them and can last into the future and be felt by children and grandchildren who come later.

There was a sweetness to the time of Elizabeth's death. She had done it exactly the way that she had wanted. It was pain free. She maintained her dignity and sense of control. She didn't have a long drawn out experience of decline, as her cancer reduced the scope of her life to her hospital bed. On the professional level as her nurse, I cognitively supported her decision and assisted as much as I was able to. And yet, personally It left me shaken and perplexed.

Elizabeth's death was a hastening of death, a suicide. In my heart of hearts, I had the feeling that the episode was violent in some essential way. That was my personal experience. I know that when I judge someone, that I am the one who pays the price of having a closed heart. Just as Elizabeth followed her path, I have to follow my own path, as it is the only one that will take me anywhere. I am the only one who can evaluate that path, just as Elizabeth was the only one who could truly know and evaluate her path.

Kathy

Kathy was a long-time personal friend whom I had lost track of for a number of years, until she called me up one day from the hospital, asking if I would come to see her. She told me how she had repeatedly gone to the emergency clinic complaining of severe pain in her neck, but that the medical staff thought that she was simply seeking drugs and had not taken her seriously. Finally, one doctor was willing to listen to her and investigate. She did a scan and Kathy was diagnosed with inoperable, terminal brain cancer.

Kathy called because she knew that she had a limited amount of time left. She had never been interested in dogma or religious opinions, but she needed something spiritual. A spiritual mentor named Hanuman Golden, once told me, *Only teach what you know.* Taking that to heart, I recounted to Kathy some of the experiences of my inner journey since we had last seen each other.

Kathy returned to her apartment to receive in-home hospice care, where I visited her regularly over the next few weeks, not as her nurse, but as a friend. As I was accustomed to do then, each morning when I arose, I would sit for forty minutes in meditation on my little black bench facing the white wall. I dedicated my practice to reducing her suffering through the compassion meditation *Tonglen*. I would contact that place inside myself where I held my relationship with Kathy. On the inhale, I would come into contact with what I perceived as her state. It felt dense and heavy, like a concentrate of a lifetime of suffering. On each in-breath, I would invite her suffering to come into my heart. Feeling it enter my heart, I would have compassion for her and for myself. On the exhale, in my mind's eye, I would direct towards Kathy a soft, opalescent light filled with peace and love.

One morning I went into my Kathy meditation as usual. But, instead of encountering the normal heaviness when I contacted her inside myself, I had a sudden feeling of supreme lightness and purity of being. It felt that all the fruits of compassion were there. The darkness and suffering were gone. An hour later, Kathy's sister called to tell me that Kathy had died in the early hours of the morning, and asked, *Would I come over?*

I went in to where Kathy's body was lying in her bed. Kathy was wearing brilliant red lipstick and fingernail polish at the time of her death. Her face was the palest white, her hands dark blue. It made a very strong impression. I began to ring my Tibetan bells. After each sound of the bell, I said, *Kathy! You are dead now. You don't need this body anymore.*

That evening, when I was ready to go to sleep, the stark image of Kathy's face stood out in sharp detail in my mind. It filled my attention, as if it were right before my eyes, exactly as it had been that morning. I began once more to do the breathing meditation, but instead of her suffering, I imagined that I was inhaling the spectre of her face. With my eyes open, I saw in my mind's eye, an inhuman creature of smoke in the room with me, in a form that I had once seen in rock art, etched by a long, long dead, prehistoric artist. I proceeded to inhale the image. The ambient light in the room went dim, as if I had cataracts. I felt as though I were looking through the eyes of Kathy's corpse. I said to her, *Kathy, you are dead now! You are welcome to stay in this emptiness that is my heart, until you realize that you are this same emptiness, just as I am. Then please go.* Immediately, the light in the room returned to normal and I could see clearly again. After that, I could remember the experience of seeing Kathy that morning, but the image of her death mask had smoothed away.

Commentary

It seemed that an element of Kathy - what element I cannot say - had attached itself to me in some way, perhaps through the same knowing, the same seeking which had inspired her to call me from her hospital room after her terminal diagnosis. My experience that evening on the day of her death, leads me to believe that whatever remained of our resonance together, still had a movement to complete, something which continued after her death and my visit to her some hours later.

I learned later, that what I had experienced was consistent with what is called *Phowa*, in some Buddhist traditions. It is the process where a living person, through their own stability in awakening, can help to usher a deceased person into the Unborn, the stateless state that is always, ever present, that was never born and does not die. It strikes me that this process of bridging between the living and the dead, is reflected in what sometimes happens in a constellation, when a representative of a dead person is able to stay present while fully available to the role they are in.

We are individuals, the collective and beyond.

Part Two

Systemic Constellation

Oryx gazella

Death in Systemic Constellation

Dr. Ursula Franke-Bryson and Thomas Bryson in Conversation

Elanus caeruleus Ursula Franke

Thomas: As a clinical psychologist, you have been studying, teaching and working with systemic constellations for almost twenty years now. As you have pointed out in previous conversations, it has never lost its attraction, poignancy and beauty for you. How do you understand constellations now?

Ursula: There are many descriptions of systemic constellation, available from many sources. For me, systemic constellation is a method in psychology where the therapist and client together create a representation of the inner world of the client by externalizing it, so that the client may have a new perspective and the therapist through this image, can have easier access to unconscious structures that define the client and his moves.

With the resource of presence and the interventions of the therapist, the client can explore this externalization, feeling, seeing, and even changing that image and integrating what is there. This helps the client to make more sense of their life, which is rooted in, based upon and connected with their inner world. When he is able to bring presence into contact with his inner structures, new information and flow enter into those otherwise hardly accessible places, and in the process changes them. This leads to greater internal integration and to the updating of old programming, so that the client can move forward feeling more complete and fulfilled, with more peace and ease of being.

T: How do you find death to be relevant for systemic constellation?

U: Death is the essential point in the center of systemic constellation. For all of us, the reality is that any day, or even any moment,

San cave painting, Erongo Mountains Namibia

may be our last. When we stop to think about our life, it is symptoms or suffering which make us reflect about ourselves in a bigger context, and then all the important questions come up: How does it come that I am where I am now? Have I lived the right way? Have I fulfilled what I was meant to do? What do I still have to do before I die, so that I can move on in peace and go happily?

At the same time, it seems that unfulfilled lives and situations around peace-less death particularly, leave a strong imprint in the body which is passed on in the lineage. It is as if the human organism keeps this information of danger, struggle and possible survival as an important biographical and trans-generational memory, for access in future similar situations, so he can react immediately in case he is exposed to such an occurrence again.

T: What do you think is the key to approaching these issues?

U: The symptoms and the questions of the client point directly to the core issue of the system, but in a symbolic way. On the one hand, we have to accompany the client in his actual experience and suffering, so that he can realize that he is not, once again, left alone confronting the most painful and difficult issue of his whole lineage. On the other hand, as facilitators, we have to open a bigger space of understanding into which this personal complaint fits in, in all its complexity and subtlety, like a missing piece in a detailed jigsaw puzzle. Working on these two levels, we can also help the client to draw a greater circle of understanding of his personal urge being both personal and not personal at the same time.

T: Then the ideal therapist or facilitator must be grounded in their own journey through life and death, to be able to walk their talk, so to speak?

U: Absolutely. Observation helps to understand, but having gone through the process on my own, brings a deeper and more compassionate understanding in a more subtle and complex way.

The best way to learn is to research your own questions and ways of being and your physical reaction patterns, how they connect with your family and lineage and their encounters with death. The whole history of the family and the country is represented there: The war experiences of the father, the early death of the siblings of the mother, seeing the killing during the revolutionary times, and further back to the burning of the witches in the villages nearby, the fear of death of the farmers during the Thirty Years War, and so on. All this is still represented in my own body. And having been there, makes one fearless, even in front of the wishes of the client to die, or of their or our own possible death by illness or old age.

When a client comes to the point of struggle between his own living and dying, their suffering has delivered them precisely to the point where they need something fresh, other thoughts, other images, new possibilities to deal with where they are stuck. The old well-known family structure is not useful anymore. It has to die to make space for a deeper, more personal expression.

If the client hasn't enough resources to resolve the situation on his or her own, we can support them to access a context in which to find the needed resources and integration.

U: What is the growing edge of your own thinking on this topic?

T: I am drawn to the confluence of spirituality and systemic constellation, where I can see how central identity is for them both. My perspective is that death means the loss of one´s own identity. Therefore, to be a potential catalyst for others, I need to be able to see through the imagined importance of my own identity, to differentiate between the personal and systemic levels of identity, and to let them both find their places within the greater wholeness. I am convinced that in order to be an effective guide to accompany another on his journey, one needs to know the terrain.

U: From your experience working in hospice, do you think that the way the dead are represented in systemic constellation comes close to the truth?

T: I think that through exploring the inner world of clients and externalizing it in systemic constellation, one gets an impression of how being dead is held in the unconscious inner world of each specific client. I take what we see in constellations to be a relative truth, which is useful for this client´s healing and integration. Whether that is the reality of being dead, there is no way for me or anyone of us to objectively know. But then, what is called objective reality, is always subjectively experienced, as reality is normally seen and interpreted through many layers of interpretation: biological, cultural and personal. The Tibetans seem to be experts on death. I would find it interesting to explore some Tibetan Buddhist philosophy on death through systemic constellation.

What is your perspective on this question? How do you evaluate the truth of the way that the dead are represented in systemic constellation?

U: As you said, this truth has many layers and it depends on us, which of them we bring into focus. I am reminded of an insightful statement I once heard from Guni Baxa. She said that when we set up a representative, for the dead grandfather for instance, that we don't really know what we actually are setting up. It seems that each representative is a doorway, which opens onto much more than a single person's experience. He is representing the grandfather with all of his own life experiences and relationships, and that of his lineage, and further back than it might seem on the first view. At the same time, he is also representing all the grandfathers, like an archaic figure, with all their personal and structural experiences.

T: This complex multi-layered aspect of representation is intriguing. Some representatives know how to be present while being open to the greater possibilities behind the identity of the one who is being represented. When their representation of the dead becomes multi-leveled, their role can become very healing. As a facilitator, I sometimes point out to the representatives, that while they are in the role, they do not have to be confined to the suffering of the role, and this changes their possibilities - and those of the client.

U: You have worked in the medical field and have researched the biological and scientific foundations of trauma, and also have a background in Buddhist meditation. How do you see these different viewpoints fitting together in your systemic thinking?

T: I don't see a gulf between spirituality and science. I find the rational, logical inquiry of science and the open-mindedness of contemplative practice to be complementary. I find them both to contribute to facilitating systemic constellation.

Engaging reality from the perspective of being the emptiness that was found in meditation and not defending one's identity, is what I came to understand to be the essence of the scientific method and the phenomenology which is spoken of in systemic constellation. This matches with the deepest moments of my own work experience, both as a facilitator and as a hospice nurse.

I take systemic constellation to be about improving the integration of specific, personal, client content within the greater impersonal context. I am aware that to reach that, I need to neither lose

Lydomorphus Beetle Ursula Franke

contact with the details of the personal content of the client, by being untouched by client suffering, nor to be so drawn into the trance structures of the client that I lose the resourcefulness of an outside position.

On the most inclusive level, systemic thinking conceptually contains: the individual, the group and the lineage of their family system within their cultural and natural environments within space and time, and still beyond.

U: Whenever there is a conceptual pair, like the duality of you and me, there is a natural implication of something greater which includes us both.

T: Yes. I like to point out that in quantum physics, light is described as having the characteristics of being both a particle, and of being a wave which is propagated within a field. The field in which the wave is propagated, is the context which is beyond and contains both the particle and the wave, and yet is not separate from them, just as we are not separate from the rest of the universe.

U: When we look at what is experienced in systemic constellation, the client's personal experience of time and space is just part of the picture. The client can be seen as an extension of the lives in the past. Those that are dead, and their experiences, have not entirely vanished from the inner world. And each of us has interconnections with others, regardless of the physical distance. That place outside of the march of time, includes those who have come before, as well as being the impersonal realm beyond the personal and systemic. And it may well include those, who come after us...

T: What meaning does this have for the work you do? How do you apply this recognition in your practical work?

U: In systemic constellation, as in many kinds of therapy, we always seek to understand the client and their symptoms within the greater context. When people and their symptoms are narrowly defined, the interconnections and complexities of reality are lost.

On the personal level of the client's lived experience, the symptom bothering him may be about having physical or emotional symptoms that do not seem to make sense to the client. When the symptom is explored, one may recognize that it is a repetition from before, which reappears in following generations. And that this pattern has its source in a traumatic, even life threatening experience in the past, perhaps by the grandmother or by an ancestor even further back. The symptom makes sense in the context of that time, but not now in the actual life of the client.

Through systemic constellation and the resource of being present, the client is able to momentarily step outside of the confines of their lineage, to look at the symptom as if from the outside, like a witness, as it is called, instead of always looking from inside and being caught and restricted by the symptom.

T: When would you consider bringing in a representative for death in a constellation?

U: When there is a high degree of intensity and breadth of trauma in the system, or when a personal or human dimension is not strong enough to bring a resource for a change, we need bigger, more impactful interventions to fit the circumstances, and to allow a new movement in the dynamic. At this point, it is helpful to bring in abstracts that are encompassing greater circles of meaning and cover the space set out by the presenting complex of the client. These abstract elements might be war, life, death, the home country or presence.

It is not unusual, when we encounter clients who are carrying in their body residues of massive traumas that are repeated over and over in different generations, that it is only through using these abstract elements that resolution for the client can be found.

T: As the living, we can't know what death is actually like, but we can externalize how death and those who have died are held in the inner world of the client. What types of experiences have you had externalizing dead people from the lineages of your clients?

U: When representatives of the client's ancestors are seen and included by the client, they are usually friendly, benevolent and interested in the client´s life and development. After all, it is their own lineage in which they are participating. In constellations there is an interchange between those who have passed on and those who are still alive, as in many traditions of indigenous peoples, as well as in historical civilizations like the Romans. The living need the protection and support of the dead ones, and the dead need the memory and care of the living ones. One might say that by honoring and seeing those who have come before us, that we turn them into ancestors. Now that they are dead, they are depending on those of us who are still in a living body, subject to will and able to act, to accomplish the things that they can no longer do while being held by death.

T: And do you find that externalized ancestors are not always friendly?

U: No, not always. Sometimes externalized ancestors are indifferent, angry, want revenge or have demands on the living, specifically on the client. Often the client refuses to respond to what is expected from him, as an embodiment of the essence of his system, but I tell them, Who else could do it if not for you? The question is, What does this person need, now that they are dead? The client at this point is just an executing medium to close a gestalt that had been left open by a presumably abrupt event that lead to the death of this person. It is as if this person has not found peace yet. And it is the client who can bring this transformation and by doing so, will turn from suffering, being haunted and victimized into an acting, responsible adult.

Naturally, as a response, the client would withdraw, as all had done before him. This is why the gestalt has not been completed, the tasks have not been fulfilled and the story has not been brought to a satisfying, peaceful ending. Confronting these negative emotions and the demands of inner voices, or of externalized ancestors, is not a well explored habit in that family, otherwise the client could do it with ease.

This relief in completion is what the whole system has been searching for, pointing out more and more urgently through symptoms, where to look and what to pay attention to.

T: Do you think that dead ancestors exist, with needs in this time and space, now?

U: With my European bias, I say that there is no way to truly know in what realm the dead belong or exist, or if they do. Many cultures have strong opinions on the topic. In some cultures, they can confidently say where the ancestors are. The *Sangoma*, or traditional shamans in southern Africa, state that the representatives of the ancestors, are the ancestors, not representatives for them. Daan van Kampenhout mentioned that the spirits of the ancestors are around us in calling distance. So when we set up representatives we call them into the body of these participants. For practical

European purposes, we can either take the perspective that the ancestors are external to the client, or that they are dwellers in the client's inner world and are externalized in the constellation. In the end, this might be the same.

T: It reminds me of the Sufi concept that while a drop of water is contained by the ocean, at the same time, the ocean is contained in each drop of water.

U: When we look systemically, the needs of the individual, the group and of the system are intertwined and reciprocal. The system needs individuals to maintain the structures which have supported the system in the past. But, it also needs those who can ensure that adequate flow and exchange occur between the individuals in the group and between the group and the greater system. We often see in practice that different family members will take different roles in the system, in terms of providing either the structures needed for safety, or to have an adequate interchange beyond the system - to bring in new blood, so to speak, to continue healthy growth and development.

The system as a whole requires the individual to mature and become autonomous, in essence, to differentiate into their own unique character and strengths, and to then be a contributing member of the system. From the individual's perspective, one needs a place within the system, and also to be seen as a unique individual who brings valuable contributions to the whole by being who they are.

T: And when there are competing needs in the system between those of the individual and of the group?

U: We can interpret symptoms as speaking of something that needs attention. The more we have explored what is called, the Interrupted Reaching-out Movement, the more apparent it becomes that difficulties in the past can lead to imbalances between the needs of the individual and the group.

The correction of imbalances or disruptions in the lineage, can be seen to be the need of the system, as represented by both the needs of the ancestors and by the living individuals in the system.

T: What do you mean by a disruption?

U: There can be many events which create breaks in the lineages that make up the system. Untimely deaths, war, trauma or the need of a population to migrate because of disease, famine or invasion are just some of them. Clues to these events in the client's background may be found in the stories, symptoms and body language of the client, as well as through exploring the genogram or by using representatives in a constellation.

For example, when an ancestor has had an untimely death, or when a client didn't personally know the ancestor, there can be a palpable void in the system which would have been filled by that person. When a father died while the child was still small, then the mother might not have spoken about him. For the child, it is as if the father and his shared life with the mother had never existed.

Reconnecting with this father, who is being represented by a participant in a constellation, or even going through the process in the imagination or with floor markers, can be done by the client looking at the father and naming the fact of the relationship, by saying something like, Look at me father, I am your son, or, I am your daughter. If the client has children, then they were also deprived of the grandfather and what came through him. For regaining the link and strengthening it, the client could say, Father, look. These are my children. Your grandchildren, and then Introducing them by name, one by one. This is to restore the union between the generations, to connect the roots that have been broken.

Sometimes when the father dies, it is as if his whole side of the family disappears for the client. Then the grandparents, great grandparents etc. might be placed behind the father to give him a background, weight and context, and can become a resourceful presence in their inner world. Through this the client can gain a sense of place and belonging.

One might say that by honoring and seeing those who have come before us, one can develop a relationship with the ancestors, who in turn can give roots and support.

T: Sometimes the representatives of dead ancestors seem to be caught in the trauma of the death of the person they are representing.

U: Yes. I discuss and comment on just such a case in the section of clinical examples, where a representative seemed to be caught up in the representation for some time afterwards.

T: Some facilitators use the concept of *soul* to organize their perceptions of what is encountered in systemic constellation. What is your perspective on this?

U: Yes, concepts are useful for organizing experience. The use of the concept soul in systemic constellation is a legacy of Bert Hellinger, who was a Christian missionary before he went on to make his mark with Family Constellation. We prefer to use terms that are not so closely identified as being part of a specific cultural identity, but which are more universal.

T: Christianity carries a cultural heritage which can easily exclude other perspectives. Soul implies something mysterious, eternal, spiritual and important. We prefer to take a purely functional perspective, that everything that is seen in a constellation is an externalization which can be understood to be part of the inner world of the client.

Instead of placing the eternal aspect of reality into the concept of soul, we prefer to point out the universality and stability found in the readily accessible sense of presence. In terms of the eternal, we prefer to ask, What is it in your own life experience that has never changed? This does not contradict the Christian view, but turns the focus onto a more commonly accessible understanding.

I remember a woman whom I had had as a patient who had once said to me, *When I look in the mirror, I see this little old lady looking back at me. I wonder, who is that? Because when I look inward, I feel that I am exactly the same as I was when I was a very small girl.*

Self-Exploration Exercises

Panthera leo Grant Reed Letaka Safaris

The reality is that

each moment our deaths grow ever closer.

What happens when one imagines that death

is sitting in the circle with us now,

listening to our conversation?

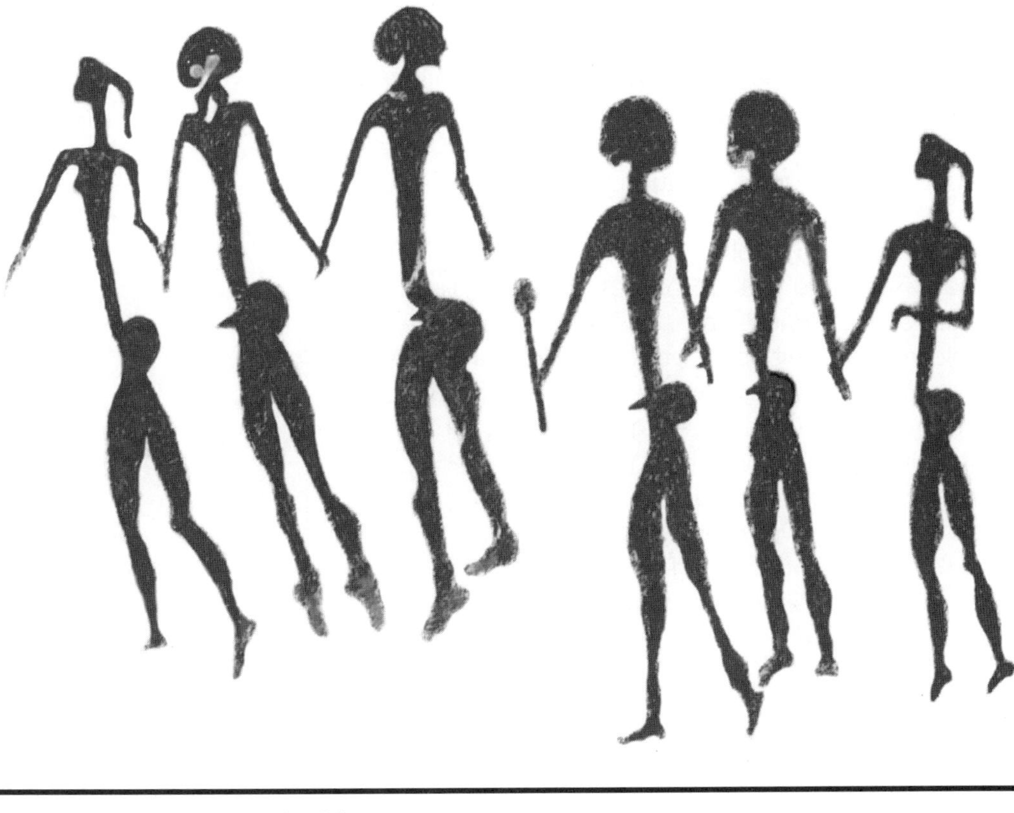

San Cave Painting, Erongo Mountains, Namibiba

Introduction

Before beginning self-exploration exercises, it is important to be aware if clients or participants have personal experiences of trauma which remain unresolved. Sometimes a relatively benign intervention, like asking a client to exhale, is enough to trigger a strong emotional response. If one is going to take someone on a journey, it is good to know the way back home! As a therapist, one has an obligation to be able to contain the results of one's interventions, to be able to take people back out of the trances which may have been triggered by our interventions.

For the reason of safety and self-empowerment, we normally start with an exercise to build resources. In trainings and in private practice, we demonstrate the Power of Presence, so that people learn in their bodies, that it is true that feeling the sensations of one's emotions is actually empowering. It may seem counter-intuitive that feeling difficult emotions is actually strengthening. If something is frightening, the natural conditioned response is to move away from it, not to go there and feel it. However, moving toward the problem is moving toward the solution. But if this hasn't been done in the system, there is no inner knowledge in the system of how to do this. As the client is the essence of the system, this approach may be foreign.

By starting with the body, we are re-introducing a sometimes forgotten way of knowing. The normal European response when facing a problem, is to look to the mind for a solution, to get more information there. In the process, one is drawing on the unconscious inherited inner library, which is supplemented by the conscious experiences of one's own life. However, in the process of focusing on the mind, one tends to be disassociated from the body. Feelings aren't called thoughts. Feelings release their treasures when they are felt, and when they are perceived as sensations, it brings one back to the here and now - the only place where functional power exists.

Death and the threat of not belonging, are normally perceived as being the most dangerous things in life. A child depends on the parents or family to protect him or her from this danger. Developing a relationship with death is the task of an autonomous adult, one who has no parents to stand between him or herself and death. Mimicking the behaviors from the past, may help a child to feel that he belongs, but seeing and belonging to oneself, is a mark of adulthood. In exploring one's relationship with death, unresolved needs of one's inner child may make themselves known. This is the good news! When one becomes conscious of someone in our inner world, one can explore what that one needs now, and then to open our hearts and strengths to that need and offer the safety, love and respect that is at the core of that one's need.

The following five exercises are offered as suggestions. Contemplating death has a very long history. There are many more possibilities and sources for this kind of exploration. These exercises are appropriate for group processes, training workshops and also for the individual practice, where you as a therapist or facilitator can take the second role. The main instruction is that both follow their own inner movement. Each process should take just a few minutes. Afterwards, there is always enough time to share and explore in more detail, what has been experienced in the exercise. These exercises in pairs, following their own movement and impulses freely to explore specific situations, are based on the work of Siegfried Essen.

1. Your relationship with Death

Set up the other person as yourself, then set up yourself as death, in relationship to the one representing you. The main instruction is to feel free to move and follow your impulses in silence. If this is done in a group setting, when you have finished, trade places and the other sets you up as them, and themselves as death. When you are finished, sit together and quietly discuss what you experienced. In the private practice, the therapist can stand in the place of the client.

Commentary

We set the client in the representation of death to facilitate their seeing themselves from a different perspective, and to understand death from the inside, so to speak. By having the client standing in the place of death, he or she experiences a greater space of peace and silence. Looking at oneself from this perspective, is often full of love, acceptance, patience and support.

People living deeply have no fear of death.

Anaiïs Nin, Diary, 1967

2. After Death

Imagine that you have already died. Then ask yourself, Now that I am dead, is there anything that I need?

Keep breathing and take some time to scan your body and mind and allow the answers to arise. What is your experience when you imagine this? You can reflect on the body, heart or mind level and find out what is important to you, now.

This process can be done in the mind's eye in either group or individual settings, or as a personal self-exploration.

Commentary

When death has already occurred, one's strategies for coping with life are no longer relevant. Imagining that one is beyond the needs for control, and have no more physical needs and can accomplish nothing more, can be extremely relaxing. As a spiritual exercise, imagining that one is already dead, but still present, opens up the possibility of recognizing oneself beyond the identity.

3. Relationships after Death

When you look at your loved ones now, what do they need from you, now that you are dead? What is it that you can offer them from where you are now. And how do you look at them from the vantage point of death?

Commentary

Looking at our companions in life from the place of death, we can look at our relationships without being bound into the needs of a living body who is defined by identity. At this point, you might transfer the knowledge gained from the experience into your actual life situation and your relationships.

4. Death as a resource

Set up a person with whom you are having a challenging relationship, or which is in some way unsettled. Set up death standing next to them. What changes? Then set up death standing next to you. What is your experience?

Commentary

This can be done in the imagination, through floor markers or with other symbolization, like a chair, cushion or a rock. We observe that the dimension that comes into a relationship through the proximity of death, changes the encounter between two people. Death reminds us of our restricted time together and of our deeper humanity. It helps to focus one on what is really important.

5. Embodied Genogram

This exercise works well in large groups, but can be adapted for use with inanimate symbols or floor markers.

The facilitator sets up a representative for each of the parents of the client, standing side by side. Behind them, place representatives for their parents. Continue setting up representatives for as many generations as you have participants for. Then imagine that behind them, there are still many, many more hundreds of ancestors.

The instructions to the representatives are: Look at the client for a moment as you go into the role, and imagine that you are representing the moment of death of the person in whose place you are standing.

After the representatives have had enough time to experience the role, have each one say one word which describes their experience, and one word for what they are needing now, if anything.

Commentary

The embodied genogram carries a great deal of information about the lineage as seen through the eyes and body of the client.

The primary uses we see, are:

Exploring the family tree for resources. Which ancestors are looking at the client with friendliness, openness, interest or love?

Identifying those who have not settled into a peaceful death yet and are still needing something. These incomplete *gestalten* can be finished through the willingness of the client to engage the issues.

Do the one word descriptions of the representatives experience in the exercise, match the client's situation or symptom in pattern or quality?

This exercise has potential for much exploration and variation, depending on the client or group needs.

Death in Systemic Constellation

Clinical examples with commentary

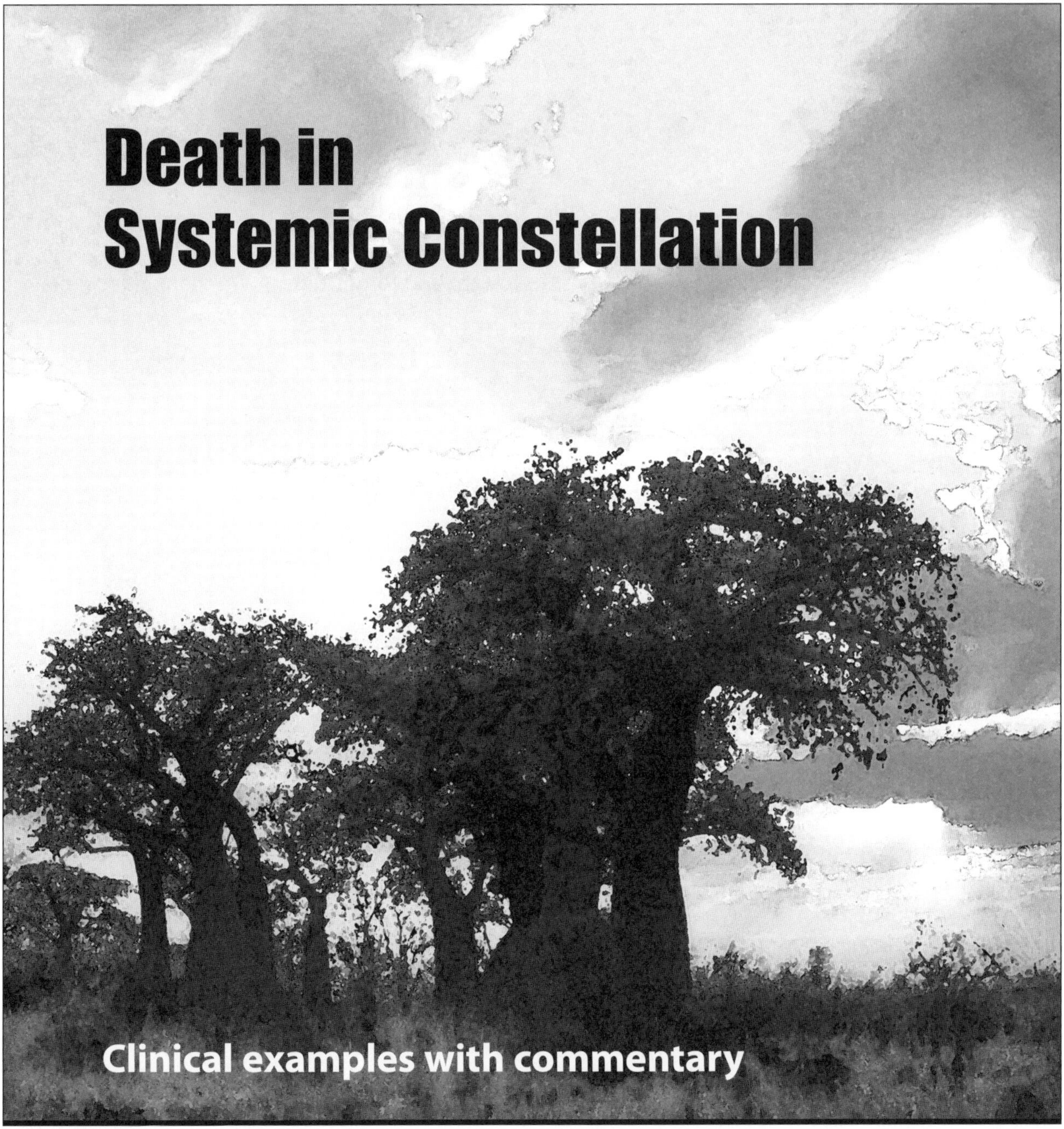

Adansonia digitata

The following ten clinical examples from practice weave a pattern with the threads of trauma. Within the field is beauty and pain, insight and forgetfulness. We thank our clients.

Reunion in Death

In this case, I was working with an Italian client through Skype, the computer program. Remote sessions through the internet or by telephone, have the advantage that we are able to work with clients from anywhere in the world, without the need to travel. On the other side, you have to be more attentive and explicit in your obervations, questions and interventions. When connecting with a client remotely, it is helpful to work slowly and take smaller steps. Nevertheless, it has proven to be a valid equivalent for sessions in person.

This client was familiar with systemic constellation and thought that perhaps there was a systemic component to the hip pain which had been increasingly calling for her attention. As the pain grew stronger, and she had been unable to resolve it through medical and physiotherapeutic means, this was her last hope.

When I asked the client to imagine a representative for the pain, she immediately described her vision of a young, emaciated, Italian soldier from the First World War. I asked her about this image and she described the man in detail:

Client: *He has come home from the war. His eyes are empty. He is gaunt and filthy. His uniform is in tatters and his feet are wrapped in rags. He is so weak he can barely stand and will collapse soon.*

Therapist: *Is the young soldier alive now?*
Client: *No, he is dead.*
T: *Now that he is dead, who or what does he need?*
C: *He needs his mother.*
T: *Is she dead now, too?*
C: *Yes.*
T: *Now that they are both dead, nothing bad can happen to either one of them anymore. They have all the time in the world to be together.*

I suggested to her an image of a peaceful place in her homeland, to give a context for the man in the image and the one he was longing for:

Imagine that the young soldier and his mother are sitting comfortably at a table on the veranda of an old country house. He is no longer hungry and dirty and she too, has no more bodily suffering. They sit together there for five or ten years, and in that time, the sun hasn't moved at all. They drink and eat delicious food for hours and never get full.

When the client spontaneously had a big exhale, her body was signaling consent, so that we could take another step in this guided visualization. I moved to reinforce the resourceful place of the young man representing her pain - and for the client.

They sit and look into each other's eyes. They hug each other and talk over what they had never been able to say during their lifetimes. They cry and feel what they had never been able to feel while alive. After a while, they laugh and smile and lapse into a timeless silence. As they sit there together in silence for another year or two, or twenty... they admire the way the sunlight is streaming through the leaves of an old tree and enjoy the sounds of birds singing.

The client smiled, still and relaxed.

In order to find a larger, stable picture, I offered her a resolution image for the young soldier within the greater collective field of trauma.

Far beyond the garden, out in the field, the mother and her son can see that there are many, many other young men there walking together. They were also soldiers once, long ago. But now they all look healthy again, walking hand in hand and singing. As they walk along, they are joined by all the other young men, the ones who had been their enemies once, so long ago. They see each other. Looking into each other's eyes, they know what only another who has gone through war knows. They welcome each other with love and respect, embracing and crying, slapping each other on the back or shaking hands, smiling, laughing or telling stories. After a while, an hour or a year, the young men seem to just fade into the field and are gone. Now it is just a field full of flowers. All are in bloom in the morning sunlight.

The client reported later, after our work together, that although her hip pain still comes and goes, that she found the image very healing.

The real story of a war, is no story at all - blackness, sadness, silence... And if I describe what I saw of the war, you'll know it from the point of view of the living, and this is the smallest part of the truth. The truth itself is what was finally apprehended by those who didn't come back.

Mark Helprin, *A Soldier of the Great War*, p. 91

Commentary

Healing images and phrases, like the ones in the constellation, come spontaneously out of the resonance within the common field shared between the therapist and the client. They are created new in each situation and follow the needs and moves of the client. As this client described the soldier in the image it felt familiar to her. She felt a connection to the brother of her Grandfather who had died on the battlefields somewhere. When she described him, I also could see him in my mind´s eye, and together we built up the healing trance.

War leaves a legacy in the inner worlds of those who are exposed to it - and beyond into the future. In many systemic constellations we see what a deep and long-lasting impact war can have. The latest epigenetic research shows that when soldiers are exposed to the trauma of war, that their neurophysiology is altered, and that trauma-related response patterns are passed on to their children.

It is unexpected, that in the imagination death is a safe place, where people are beyond the fear, trauma and pain which has played such a strong part in human conditioning. Accessing this place after death, gives more space in the inner world of the client, whereby the people in the inner representation can finish what they haven't said, felt, or encountered with each other during their lifetimes.

The structure which we use when leading a guided visualization is as follows:

Finding an inner image arising out of the symptom - the young man;

Evoking a more detailed description of the image - the young man's physical and emotional state;

Context for the scene - meeting beyond fear and pain in death;

Time for emotional development of the client - given through pacing by the therapist;

The needed resource for the person in the image - the young man in the image being seen, first by the client, then by his mother;

Completion of his emotional process - the interaction between the mother and son; sometimes between client and son, when the client becomes the mediating source of change;

Expanded context - the completion of the emotional process gives a resourceful basis for looking at the collective trauma in a larger context - the other soldiers and their enemies, and

Resolution - a final image of peace in a natural setting, as nature is a deeply known, reliable resource.

We follow this structure to give relief of the symptom, by finding an inner image, altering it and bringing it to a long searched for, good end. It seems that the symptom acts like a messenger from this longing for solution. It brings attention to the unconscious representation of the emotional content, which we have come to consider as real events somewhere in the lineage of the client.

However, it may well be also a symbolic representation of archaic structures of the inner world, of the architecture of the human brain, a part of the collective unconscious as C.G. Jung described it. Treating these structures on a symbolic level gestalt therapy delivered good outcome in the practice.

As we do not have capacity to draw this distinction, we can treat it as being both at the same time: unconscious memories from the lineage of the client and archaic symbols, which may actually be the same.

In this case, the healing image arose from the question for completion, Now that he is dead, who or what does he need? The longing in the family system is fulfilled in the image of the mother and son together, and for the greater picture of those who had shared the same experience, like with the other soldiers and their former enemies. This expanded context gives a supportive background for the client's path of transformation. Through this process, that is close to interventions from hypnotherapy, the final picture has become a detailed open space, that will be able to replace the former tightness of the inherited trauma trance.

A tension in the neck

A woman in a training seminar came forward wanting relief from her symptoms. For many years, she had been suffering both insomnia and tension headaches, which normally originated in her neck. She had tried many different approaches to reduce the tension and get relief from the insomnia, but nothing really resolved it. Each new medication she tried would work for only for a short while, then the symptoms would return. She always felt somewhat exhausted and depressed from lack of sleep, and was frustrated by her inability to be done with it.

In this training group, we had taught the exercise demonstrating the Power of Presence, how feeling emotions as bodily sensations is empowering, rather than dissociating into the mind and thinking about them. I asked the client what she had experienced during the exercise. I felt afraid, she said. But, I can't even come close to feeling my fear. It is just too much.

Because her symptoms were of long duration, without any conscious, causal event in her lifetime, we assumed that it had a context from some time before. Fear is always at least partially a systemic pattern, as fear has been with us since the dawn of humanity. And because her fear was so great, a simple hypothesis presented itself; that the tension was related to an inherited trauma-related pattern, and that fear would be an entry point to where the trauma pattern was held in her inner world.

As the client was unable to approach her fear, it seemed better to use a representative for her. In this way, the client could stay a witness of the process, observing the developments shown by the representative, while keeping a safe distance.
Working as a couple we have the advantage that one can focus his attention fully on the process unrolling through the surrogate and representatives, while the other one takes care of the client, using interventions taken from body and holding therapy to ease and support her during the process.

I asked for a volunteer from the group, someone who might already be feeling the client's fear. After looking into the eyes of the client, the representative reported what she was perceiving in her own body.

Representative of client: *I feel like something is pulling my head backward.* She bent her neck sharply back and to the side. *My throat is constricted and my breath is being cut off.*

Facilitator: *What do you feel below that?*

R: *I can't feel anything below my abdomen.*

F: *When you imagine that you are looking down at your feet, in your mind's eye, what do you see?*

R: *My feet don't touch the ground.*

F: *Is this person a man or a woman?*

R: *A man.*

F: *How old is he?*

R: *Maybe nineteen.*

Because of the potential for strong arousal in the client, I didn't go further into the trauma image. Instead, I skipped ahead to the future and asked the client's representative,

F: *Does this person live or die?*

R: *He dies.*

F: *Now that he is dead, who or what does he need?*

R: *He needs his father. He needs to be seen and forgiven for failing.*

I asked for a male volunteer to stand as a representative of the father of the young man in the image, and directed him to say to his son: *"I see you. I am your father, no matter what."*

Hearing this, the client burst into tears, but after some minutes, she calmed down. This was the primary releasing emotion. Unlike secondary emotions, which have no apparent causal event and then tend to stay at the same level, this emotion had a triggering event, rose quickly to a peak and then subsided. This primary engagement with the emotions, was the new information that the system needed.

I asked the client to let the representatives come out of their roles, by touching each one and calling them by name. I asked her to find a seat between the woman who had represented her and the man who had represented the father of the person in the image. The client agreed readily to sit with them and to be held by them both until our next break.

Later that day, I asked the client how she was doing. She smiled and said, I feel like my face is melting. I am finding all sorts of unfamiliar muscles in my face as it relaxes. Several months later, I saw the client during another module of the training seminar. She looked quite different. The brittleness was gone, her face was more expressive and she seemed to be shining from inside. I asked how she was. She smiled and said, I have been sleeping every night completely through without using any sleeping medication at all! And I rarely have any trouble with headaches.

Commentary

Just as it is with normal empathy, when one can feel what another is feeling, or know what the intention of a body movement is when seen in another, it is one of our most valuable tools, for a therapist to be able to access the client's trance. Freud named this capacity in therapeutic sessions, countertransference. This can be through sensations in one's own body, emotions or through images that arise during the interaction with the client. It seems to be a similar process for a representative who is 'in the field' of the client and can access information from there. Perhaps research into mirror neurons and the physiologic basis for empathy, will shed more light on this phenomenon in the future.

His ship sinks and in its place move the ocean waves.

Jalal al-Din Rumi

The description of the surrogate's body sensations and images, created a familiar picture for me, which I had explored many times before. With her head held at a sharp angle, breath cut off, no sensation below the diaphragm and the feet not touching the ground, it seemed that the representative was in the trauma-trance of a person who had died by hanging. The surrogate said later that it seemed to her to be a suicide by hanging, but I didn't want to place interpretations on the image. It is more precise and echoes deeper for the client when she comes to a conclusion herself.

The representative knew at once, precisely what the represented person was needing, and I followed his words. It turned out to be corresponding with the client's deep desire. The healing sentences that I asked the representative of the father to say, were simple statements of fact, that cannot be negated.

If the source of a symptom is conscious, it can usually be solved without resorting to therapy. Here the conscious knowledge had been lost. It seemed to be something shameful from a time in the past, which had occurred and been repressed and forgotten. The body remembered what the mind could not.

When a symptom has been with a client for a very long time and doesn't have a any apparent causal event, one can assume that it comes from before. When one finds the place in the body where this information is located now, an image or other perceptions related to the trauma will often arise. Then one may externalize this information into a constellation, either in the mind's eye, with ground anchors or using representatives, and develop it from there.

Body therapy schools, like Focusing by Gendlin or ..., teach five different levels how to approach a symptom: through feelings, body sensations, images, commentary thoughts and describing perceptions. I learned the technique of converting emotions into body sensations and then into images in a workshop with a colleague, Mark Wolynn. He had been working with past-life regression therapy and then applied the technique to systemic constellation.

For protecting the client from retraumatization through too high level of arousal that would demand all of her attention, we use a representative who takes over in the process. This is similar to what happens in a normal representation in a constellation, but is more focused.

Sometimes it may be useful to use the same technique to further unpack the physical manifestations that arise in representatives in a constellation, as has been done by Hellinger and others.

Finding Distance

In our training groups and individual practices, we often use focused, one-on-one exercises to explore specific themes. We also use, in the mind's eye, guided visualization to help clients come into contact with the field of their system and what they might be needing for completion or resolution. In groups, we have each participant come into contact with their own current physical and emotional state, then, imagining his or her own mother, and observe what changes. The constellation in the mind's eye is expanded, through adding one by one a person in the background that the mother might be needing, or having difficulty with, such as the grandmother or the great grandfather. With each change, the participants continue monitoring their inner changes. Later, we repeat the process with the father.

After we had done this exercise, a woman came forward because she wanted to find a more peaceful place within her relationship with her father. He was getting old now and she had not spoken with him for more than ten years. She was German and had moved to many different countries before settling in South America. She had been trained in a number of professions, but had always lost interest before she could reach success. Also, her relationships tended to be short and unfulfilled. There was good natured laughter about how she had chosen the most distant place she could find to escape her father's spell as she put it, going so far as to emigrate to a distant continent. And still, despite putting physical distance between them, she was continuously dealing with him. She fought against her similarity with him and argued with his well-known voice inside herself. She felt heaviness and exhaustion in her body, particularly when she had been thinking of him, or had recently talked with her siblings, through which she had come into touch with her family field.

To begin, we set up representatives for the client and her father. The father twisted his torso, stared blankly and finally, turned away. We brought in his parents as a potential resource and to add context, but from them, he also turned away, groaning and covering his face. His grandparents and further family members were added, but also proved to give him no comfort. Instead, his body contorted in apparent pain, he moved to the other side of the room and looked into the distance.

The client then told us that her father had been in the Second World War. He had been fighting in several battles and had been taken as a Russian prisoner of war after the devastating battle of Stalingrad. When he came home in the mid 1950's, he was a silent, violent loner. We set up representatives for his war background and his comrades. But instead of this background context giving some relief, as we often experience with war-related situations, it made him more tense and increased his obvious discomfort. It seemed that there was no place of refuge for him in this life.

What was missing for completing the picture? We put in a representative for Death. With a moan of relief, the father moved towards him and fell motionless into death´s embrace. After some time, he looked into the eyes of death, as if death were his only rescue and hope. All the representatives exhaled in relief, while the client cried silently, deeply moved. Only after her father had rested in the arms of death for a long time, could he start to notice his surroundings and begin to have some eye contact with the other representatives in the constellation. We put the daughter into the constellation, to stand next to the woman who had been representing her. The daughter was drawn to approach her father, but she also needed to keep her distance, saying, This will take some time.

Commentary

When a child moves away from her family field, in this moment it is the best thing she could do. The urge to withdraw is a precise regulating reaction to what the child perceives as overwhelming or dangerous coming from the family field. Unconsciously in the beginning, it gives discomfort in many ways, tension, inner pain, fear, repulsion that the child can not explain or even name.

It is perceived as coming from the parents on a personal level, which hinders the understanding that it might - also - be coming through the parents from events further back. And the child perceives that correctly and is not yet able to safely withstand this and to protect his or her own identity. Like in the fairy tale, the child has to leave to lose its fear, to learn skills and become independent, so that then it can come back, as an adult, and contribute this learned wisdom to the whole. If there is support from the parents, the child will learn within the family context to grow into an adult. If there is too much left unresolved, the child feels overwhelmed by their force and withdraws.

Trying to find distance is a natural reaction. But when one has internalized the trauma and its suffering aftermath, creating greater physical distance is only the first step. The inner child is stuck in a dilemma. While she wants to move away, she still longs for connection with the essence of the inner structure from which she has moved. Relief comes through creating appropriate boundaries that allow interchange without being overwhelmed by what one faces.

Sometimes dying is the best end of the story and the right thing to do, like a fire that cleanses, burning away the impurities and leaving behind possibilities for future growth.

Parabuthus schlechteri Ursula Franke

I was afraid before that.

A young woman came forward in a systemic constellation training in Africa, to overcome her fear. When working with an unfamiliar client, I normally ask if he or she had experienced any trauma in their own life, as the client's biographic trauma response may be triggered by approaching the trauma in her system. If the client has experienced trauma, it may be better to resolve that before going further.

When I asked the client about trauma in her personal biography, she described a very intense episode when she was a small girl. The house and garden where she lived with her extended family, had been invaded by armed robbers. A friend of the family had resisted them and had been shot. The client had heard one robber tell the others to grab the children and to use them as hostages. She described how she had run up and down the stairs, hiding under the table, running all over searching for a safe place. She ran into the garden to hide, and had finally escaped the robbers.

I noticed that I was holding my breath and exhaled.

Then she said, *But, I was afraid before that.*

The client then described how one morning she had awakened from a dream, but the dream didn't stop. She had gone into a trance-vision, where she was seeing her brother lying next to her in bed, completely engulfed in flames. She went into an altered state. Her perceptions became unstable and for a time she was disoriented. She said, *Since that time, I have always felt fear.*

The client was leaning away from me, so I moved my chair a bit to increase our physical separation. She had shallow breathing and a slight tremor in her hands. Her face was blushing and I could see tension in her posture. Because of her level of arousal, I decided to use a representative, instead of exploring the trance more deeply with her directly. We have the advantage of working in two; my partner used her proximity and simple physical touch to reassure the client.

The representative for the client came and sat next to the client, and at my request, looked into her eyes. She said that she could feel the client's fear, but that she herself was not afraid of feeling it. I encouraged her to scan her body and feel how the client's fear affected her, starting from her throat and slowly working down through her chest, abdomen, pelvis and legs. It is helpful to take the time needed, so that the representative and the client can feel into the process.

The representative found an image arising from the emotions, which we then externalized and explored:

Therapist: *When you imagine that you are looking down at your feet, what do you see?*

Representative for the client: *I am barefoot. I am outside in the forest.*

T: *How old is this person?*

R: *I am a young man, perhaps fourteen years old.*

With no further prompting, the representative described what she was experiencing in the trance:

R: *I am with a group of people. We are running through the forest, fleeing the village. We are all dirty, wearing torn clothing. The village has been burned. They are chasing us. My parents have already been killed. They want to kill us all. I trip on a tree root and fall.*

T: *Does the young man live or die?*

R: *He dies.*

I took a volunteer representative for the young man in the image. The representative went immediately into an intense trance state. His breathing was labored and he became pale. He didn't seem to see his surroundings and his body was in tension. I went to him and touched him, saying:

T: *It is alright.The person you are representing is already* dead. *He is safe. Nothing can hurt him anymore.*

I encouraged him to lie down and added a group of six other volunteer representatives for his family. They held his head, hands and feet, to reinforce that he was safe, saying, We are holding you now. You are safe with us now. Soon, he was relaxed, breathing normally, and his color returned.

As the representative of the person in the image who had been traumatized, had found a good place for himself, I shifted to working with the representative of the client, and then with the client herself.

T: *What does he need now that he is dead?*

R: *He needs to be remembered.*

Therapist to client: *Now that this young man is with his family again, imagine that they are now cleaning his body, combing his hair and anointing him with scented oil. They have dressed him in fine, hand-made clothing. Can you imagine a special place in the forest? Where it is peaceful and there are many birds, where there is water nearby and the light is just right?*

C: *Yes, I even know a place from my childhood, where I always loved to sit on my own.*

I expanded the image in a guided visualization:

T: *Imagine that his family is all together and that they are carrying him to this special place in the forest for his burial, to this special place in your heart. There is a procession following behind the family carrying the young man. The whole village is there with them, old and young. They are all dressed in their very best clothes. Behind the procession, all the ancestors of the whole village who have already died, are also following.*

The client deeply exhaled, showing that her body was in agreement.

T: *The family places special flowers and sweet smelling herbs around the young man's body. All those who have died before, are very interested in what is going on. They watch closely, commenting to each other on how beautiful the young man is dressed, how well all the proper rituals are being done, and how even the forest birds are wearing their best feathers.*

I said to the client: *Now that he is ready to be buried, go over to him and kneel beside him* (his representative). *Put your hand over his heart and look at him. Say to him: "I don't know who you are, but my body remembers you. Thank you."*

Sitting on the floor next to the representative, with her hands on his chest, she repeated the phrase. She thanked us, and appeared to be glowing with a new calmness and dignity, as she returned to her place in the circle of participants.

Commentary

It is good for me to remember to always tread lightly with people. One doesn't know what is in the inner world of another, what the experience of their lineage has been. We are all multi-dimensional beings, with unique histories. The trauma image which had been stored in the client's inner world, and then accessed through a representative of the client, appeared to be a fight from many years ago. Although that was never spoken about directly in the group, the client had indigenous ancestry and episodes of repeated internecine warfare in African history are well known.

As in the previous example, if it seems that the client is already in a trance, it seems adequate to not take them deeper, but enable them an experience where they can deal with the trance instead of being taken away by it. We find that using a surrogate works well for this purpose.

When the inner image reaches a point where trauma is involved, one can skip over the trauma and move beyond the moment of the death of the person in the image. Taking the time to paint a word picture from a spontaneous healing image, allows the image to grow within the client, and to overwrite the inherited trauma-related inner structure.

Sometimes what is missing in the system is a final piece of dignity, of finding a place for the one who had died traumatically and to find rest and respect in death. When one imagines that one is remembered by the living after one has died, then the fear of the loss of identity is diminished. It no longer feels like the end of one's world. Rather, one can imagine that if one's descendants remember one, that one can take one's place as an ancestor, that even though one is dead, that one belongs and has a role. By giving that dignity to the dead, the living are dignified.

At the station

A participant in a training, suddenly stood up from the small group process she was in and quickly left the room. I followed and found her in the kitchen. Her eyes were not focusing on anything to which I had access, as if she were absorbed in something in her inner world She did not respond when I spoke to her. Her upper body was contorted with muscular tension, her face a mask. Her body posture changed abruptly, accompanied by wordless sounds. She seemed to be tightly held in a trance state, presumably from some previous trauma, either biographic, inherited or both.

Knowing her for some years, I put my arms around her and held her in a tight embrace, to give her a physical container which was stronger than what was holding her. My face was close in front of her. Her head moved rapidly back and forth and she uttered a brief cry. I smiled at her, calling her by name and saying gently, I'm holding you now. You are safe. Come out! Look into my eyes! Look here in my eyes now.

Momentarily her attention was drawn to my eyes, and she seemed to see me. Then she went back into another episode of physical tension and struggle, lost focus and began again making guttural sounds. Her symptoms seemed too strong for the actual situation, so I assumed that they were related to some other place and time.

I repeatedly brought her attention back to my eyes and voice, gently calling her by her name and saying, Look at me! Stay here with me. Everything is alright now. I'm holding you now.

She alternated between the trance state and being in contact with me, looking into my eyes. Each wave of repeated tension was less intense and lasted a shorter time than the one before. With each cycle between trance and presence, she was more able to maintain my eye contact and relax a little more.

When she was able to be present, she spoke coherently;
I can feel the train rumbling in the ground. It is coming.

Then she went back into tension and struggled, saying,
It's loud. It's all black. I feel the impact. It's hitting me. There is pain.

She let out a short shriek, and then relaxed, as I continued to hold and comfort her.

She looked into my eyes, looking quite tired, but present. In a normal voice, she said, It was the suicide of my sister. I was in her body.

Her sister had been at the station and gone under a fast train. She was dragged and crushed to death.

Some months later, the client reported that she had been much more aware of her body and feeling more relaxed since that session together. She was relieved to be out of that spooky place that she knew so well, but that she never had been able to grasp or understand. She now could say that the trance had been so overwhelming and had taken hold of her so fast, that she did not have time to perceive what was happening to her.

Commentary

One's body understands what another is experiencing through feeling some of the other person's state. A therapist needs to be able to access the client state through observation and empathy, and yet to still maintain a position of resourcefulness. If one goes too far into the trance with the client, resourcefulness can be lost and one is unable to formulate an appropriate intervention.

Without training, it can be frightening when someone goes into an intense state. It is a helpful skill for a therapist to know how to be present while feeling intense emotions, to recognize one's own trance states and know how to come out of them. When working with trauma, it is important to know how to bridge between the client's trance state and this here and now.

The physicality of the client's trance state, suggested the intervention of giving the client a physical container. Holding in this way, parallels the safe embrace of a parent when a child is in distress. As the client pendulated in and out of the trance state, like one might do with systematic desensitization or in the Somatic Experiencing techniques of Peter Levine, each wave of arousal was less than the one before. And with each return to relaxation, the client became more resourceful and could better perceive without being overwhelmed. By bringing presence into contact with her inner structures, the inner complex was altered. The tight windings of taken over desperation, fear and pain could relax, allowing her to unpack the information and integrate the experience in a new way. She developed a relationship with the storm, without having to see through the eye of the maelstrom, allowing her body to find a new state.

Interestingly, this trauma-related trance was not inherited. Neither was the trauma experienced directly, nor witnessed. Still, the trauma pattern was held in her body. In a surprisingly short session, her lived experience included more ease.

Stigmochelys pardalis

Your ancestors are waiting

In a training, I once set up the story of a client's father from the Second World War, that reflected in physical symptoms in the client and in her family. I had set up several people for those involved as victims, and all had come to peace, except for one woman who stood for a Polish girl. Her situation seemed outstanding. We didn't have more information, except through the field of the client as externalized in the representatives, which showed that she had been killed in brutal, excruciating circumstances.

The dead girl was angry and demanding. The sentences the client had said to her were, I honor your death. I am sorry that your death was so difficult. You always have a place in my heart. But nothing would really settle the uproar in the woman. After the client bowed in front of her, I finished the constellation.

When I came back six months later for the next training group, the woman who had been the representative for the Polish girl, was still in the trance of the role. She had passed through hard times with sleeping disorders and depressive states, even suicidal thoughts. She was so caught in the identification with the victim that it had not even crossed her mind to call me to give her support to help her change her state. So I set her up again as the girl, with whom she was still in resonance. After tuning in and getting into contact with the scene,

I had the client speak firmly to the Polish girl and say, *You are dead now. It is all over.*

This made the Polish girl hesitate in her demanding posture. I had the client say with a strict voice, *Your dead ancestors are waiting for you. Go to rest with them.*

Again, there was a slight move. I brought in the Polish parents and grandparents and made the girl look at them. Slowly, like someone waking up and recognizing her family for the first time, she moved towards her ancestors, who were holding out their arms to receive her. As she moved, the whole group held their breath, one woman cried, and many were taken by sadness and relief. We could all still feel that the process hadn't been completed yet, but the client who had represented her, felt freed. I asked all the participants, if they would support this dead Polish girl with their thoughts and open hearts over the next several months, while she made her way home.

Commentary

I understood this dead girl to be representing more than her own personal experiences of death and of her disrupted longing for a place to belong. It seemed that many more people were involved in this process. It felt that there were complex dynamics of non-inclusion showing up, and that her slow movement was representing many more people than only herself. This could explain why speaking personally to her was not enough, and why her movements were so slow.

The image of the ancestors waiting for the dead Polish girl resonated with experiences in hospice. It was fairly common that people who were near death, would experience their dead parents and beloved ones being in the room with them. The reports from the patients were always positive, how their ancestors were reassuring and encouraging them that they would be welcome to join them.

It crossed my mind, that this felt like some restless soul or hungry ghost grasping the opportunity of joining a willing living human, and by uncovering the symptoms, she calls for resolution. I heard a tape of Felicitas Goodman, where she describes how the Catholic church deals with possessions. And how other cultures handle the different kinds and qualities and manifestations of spirits. She describes that there are different developmental stages of spirits, some insightful, so that they are reachable through explanation, but others are stubborn and crude, and have to be treated more roughly and commanded to their places like a dog. It is interesting and helpful to read fairy tales about the wandering ghosts, the unsettled spirits like *the Flying Dutchman*, or the ghosts in castles or houses. And the solutions that are offered in the Fairy Tales, how their lost souls can be redeemed: They need just one who loves them.

That's my sentence!

I was sitting in my hospice office one Monday morning. Suddenly, I felt strong tension in my abdomen and a sense of anxiety. There was always a certain amount of anxiety at the hospice, particularly on Monday morning, before the nurses learned what had happened over the weekend, and what we might be facing that day. But this anxiety was stronger than that. Because of my understanding that through feeling the anxiety as a sensation, that I would be empowered, I began to explore the feeling of the anxiety more deeply.

As there did not seem to be any apparent source for the sensations, I asked myself, *Well, what is the worst thing that could happen?* I immediately became aware of a short, emotion-laden sentence. It was, If I don't do it just perfectly, someone is going to die. I was working with death and dying at the time, but the sentence didn't make sense in that context. Death in hospice wasn't something to avoid, it was the normal outcome for my patients. While it was conceivable that I could negligently cause someone's death, my work wasn't about being perfect. It was about doing the normally expected level of professional care.

I had the intuition that the anxiety and the sentence that went with it, had come from my father. The next time I went to visit him, I met with him in private. I said to him, *Dad, I am proud to be your son.*

He had a big smile.

I am just like you, but instead of exploring the outer world successfully through science the way you have done in your career, I have been using similar thought processes, but applying them to the inner world, instead.

Then I told him about the anxiety episode I went through in my office and about the sentence that I had found.

When I said, *"If I don't do it just perfectly, someone is going to die"*, his face tightened and he burst into tears.

He blurted out, *That is my sentence!*

He then told me a story which I had never heard, about the time when he was a twenty-two year old captain in the US Army Air Force during the Second World War. He was a meteorologist responsible for making weather forecasts for the US forces as they fought across the Pacific islands toward Japan. The pilots were based on aircraft carriers and flew bombing runs against distant targets. If the winds were not as favorable for their missions as had been expected, the pilots exhausted their fuel, and would have to ditch their planes into the ocean and die. Literally, if he did not do his work just perfectly, someone would die.

Then he told me of a time in December of 1942, when he had made a forecast that a particular tropical storm was going to take an unusual course and put the US 7th Fleet into danger. He reported his forecast to the Admiral in charge of the fleet. The Admiral was not inclined to alter the disposition of his fleet on the basis of the say-so of a mere captain in the weather service. However, my father's forecast was correct. What ensued was the worst naval disaster in US naval history, including the deaths of over 750 men. All the years since 1942, logically or not, my father had felt emotionally responsible for their deaths, because he could not convince the admiral of the accuracy of his weather forecast.

I asked my father, who was 87 years old at the time, *Now that those men are all dead, what do they need now?*

He said through his tears, *They need to be remembered.*

I replied, *Those who haven't been there, can't understand. But you were there.*

He looked at me, acknowledging my statement.

And when you tell me this story, you are remembering them, aren't you?

He had a little crooked smile, and said, *Yeah.*

The next day, my niece said to me, *What happened to Grandpa? He is so much softer today than he was yesterday!*

Commentary

This is a case where the healing of a constellation was accomplished, without actually doing a constellation.

The inherited trance material in the son was experienced and traced back to its immediate source, as one might in a systemic constellation. As the son, I was able to say phrases to my father to reinforce our relative positions, while being an adult - as I might have with representatives. My father was the person who would more logically feel the anxiety that I had been feeling. With my intervention, he was able to connect to the circumstances where the anxiety made sense, and then, to feel the grief which was underneath the anxiety. Together we were able to re-frame the situation from the past, and both he and I were relieved.

By shifting the time frame away from the instant of the traumatic deaths, into this moment, my father was able to leave his repeated recriminations over what could have been done differently. He found an emotional solution for himself and for his son in the process. I was thrilled that I could bring my expertise in this area to bear on an old pain which had been bothering my father for over 65 years. And at the same time, lessened my own burden of perfectionism

Seeking Peace on Earth

A workshop participant was interested in experiencing a constellation. I asked her what she wanted to explore, and she said, I want peace on Earth.

Paradoxically, the shortest route to something may be in the opposite direction.

Facilitator: *What is the worst thing that you can imagine? Can you feel it in your body?*

I asked her to skip over any description of what she thought the worst thing was, and to simply focus directly to her body sensations. She did a mental body scan, checking her sensations from the neck down to her legs.

Client: *My throat is constricted and I have a very bad taste in my mouth. I am having trouble breathing and I would like to vomit. There is tension in my legs.*

F: *What do you see, if anything?*

C: *I am in a darkened room. There are many people crowded together, screaming. They would like to run, but there is nowhere to go.*

As she described her feelings and the image that was arising,

I could see it in my mind's eye. I didn't say anything to her at the time, but to me it seemed like an image that was from the inside of a gas chamber.

I was unsure which direction to take, so I sought to find information from the field. I asked her to set up a representative for herself. The woman representative stood and then tipped her head towards one side.

Representative: *I have the strangest feeling. It is as if one side of my body is abnormally large, and the other side is abnormally small. I feel as though I need to tip my head towards the side that is smaller.*

The client looked incredulous.

Client: *Really! I have been doing yoga for thirty years and I have always had trouble with standing balance postures. I always feel like I have to remind myself to hold my head straight, as it always seems to want to tip to one side!*

I set up the family of the client, who had been born in Germany and emigrated to North America after the war, where she had married a Jewish man whose family had been decimated by the Nazi genocide. The representatives of her family appeared to be overwhelmed and in shock. They seemed numb, unable to report any feelings. They didn't look at each other, unable to come into contact with the other representatives, including the ones I had placed for the victims of that era. In the course of the constellation, I directed the family to look at each other. They became able to see each other, and through that contact, to regain their ability to feel themselves and to perceive the others. Only when they could feel their own pain, did they become able to also see the other victims of the Nazis. And only then, was there a movement towards reconciliation amongst the representatives, and an eventual settling of the constellation with a peaceful solution where all had a place of respectful belonging.

Commentary

Peace on Earth is a large topic. When a topic is not directly personal, but encompasses a larger dimension, it is an indication that there has been a trauma which went beyond the scope of one individual, or of a single family. It is always good to keep in mind historical events that have affected an entire cohort of a population. Here it seemed that the system was trying to resolve an immense trauma through this one individual, and her personal search to reduce suffering and awaken to her deepest nature. This is reflected in the expressed desire of the client.

Because this participant was quite resourceful, I chose to use a provocative question and asked, What is the worst thing that you can imagine? I wanted to switch from the intellect and encourage the client to feel it in her body, so that I could work directly with her on that level.

However large the topic, it is always experienced personally. Consciously, the client wanted to bring peace to the world. However, unconsciously she was also trying to bring peace to the family system. To do that, it appeared that she had sought a context large enough to contain the trauma.

The route to world peace for this client seemed to come through unconsciously attempting to resolve the holocaust in the only way she could - on the personal level - by marrying a Jew, carrying the imbalance in her body and seeking to integrate the unresolved past of her system and the massive trauma beyond her family system. The more resourceful she becomes, the more she has to offer both her family system and the world.

The evening after the workshop, I got a report from the participant. She said that now she was able to perform a standing balance postures in yoga that she had been struggling with. It seems that some internal integration had taken place as a result of our co-creation. As I write this, she is on a nine-day silent meditation retreat with the Zen master Adyashanti.

Spiritual seeking often looks for new information in a realm outside of psychology and the family system. It is normal that spiritual seeking, like other seeking, has at least some of its roots in the search of the system. It is the role of each child in a family system to bring what is needed to the system, both in supporting existing structures and in bringing new flow into the system. Sometimes, when a family is metaphorically lost in the wilderness, the absolutely best thing for the family, is for one member to go for help, to seek resources, or to find a refuge outside of the structures in which the family is trapped.

Seeking resources in the realm beyond identity, in the Unborn, can be exactly what the system needs. Each system needs a method of self-reflection in order to update old programming, that may be so far out of touch with current reality, as to be dangerous to the system. The essence of therapy is to bring the client into contact with the structures of the inner world in a way that he or she can remain resourceful. The addition of greater presence to the system tends to optimize the balance of structure and flow, to help maintain safety while encouraging a primary interchange with life.

When an individual brings their growth and maturity back into the family system, the system is changed. However, the change to the status quo may well not be welcome to those who have the task of supporting the existing structures. In the story of the Prodigal Son, the son leaves home on his quest seeking the Holy Grail. He returns home a changed, more mature man. While he is welcomed by the father, he is not welcomed by the jealous brother who was interested in inheriting the kingdom.

When spiritual seeking is used as a coping strategy for avoiding the messiness of one's incarnation, the seeking may simply create a more polished, spiritualized identity. If the seeker stays identified with the new purified 'me,' there is limited new information coming to the system. The basic survival instincts which fuel the ego structure are still intact and operational, only in the new spiritual guise. What is needed, is for identity to be seen for what it really is, as part of the self-preservation instinct, and for the survival based structures to be radically updated.

Instead of finding the treasure and bringing it as a gift to the king to adorn his throne, one needs to give the king to the treasure to see if he has any real further use. The treasure of presence is a resource for the individual and family. More radical, is to see how the individual incarnation is a gift to the greater one. Then one's personal transformation can serve the whole.

There is a collective human need for a revolution of consciousness, to come into alignment with consciousness itself. When one steps out of one's identity and is absorbed into presence, all the ancestors sigh in relief, saying, At last, someone was willing to let their sense of self die, so that we could all truly live! That willingness to let the identity die, is the sacrifice of Christ, to metaphorically die so that one can find that which does not die, and then be able to truly live.

Losing One's Head

The client had sat down between us in a large training and immediately gone into a fathomless trance. We attempted to come into contact with him in the here and now, but were unable to reach through whatever was layered on him, keeping him sequestered. For over an hour we tried to build resources for him in the dramatic events of his family lineage, applying all our knowledge - it seemed in vain. We sought to establish an order within a greater context which would release the client from his trance, with no stable response. It was only when I used a strong body holding technique to give the client physical containment, that he could finally look into my eyes directly and was then unable to resist coming back into here and now. He smiled deeply and was content, although we had not resolved anything. It felt like an unconscious prelude to test our tenacity, to see if we were impressed or disabled by the dimension of his trance and symptoms.

Clients are complex beings with complex histories, which sometimes must be sifted through layer by layer. In the next years, the client went through several deep processes with us. In that time, he became more resourceful, personable and animated. In the last process, his presenting symptom was a sharp, cutting pain in his neck. We asked a very experienced participant, one who is able to stay present while exploring the trances of others, to represent him. He agreed to stand for the client and went into the role. He reported from the client's trance-field, that he felt that he was a prisoner who was now to be executed by having his head cut off.

I turned to the client sitting next to me and asked, *How is it having your head cut off?*

C: *I don't want to stay here. I want to fight, or to run away as fast as I can.*

T: *I suggest that you try simply staying present while imagining that your head is being cut off.*

He agreed.

He stood with the representative behind him so that he could feel his warmth and support. Then he entered the image of losing his head. He seemed, as if he were looking into a great distance.

Finally, he smiled and said, *I feel great!*

T: *If you can stay present while you are having your head cut off, you don't need to ever worry about trauma.*

I'll tell you a story now which I was once told. It is a story about a Chinese warlord who lived over two thousand years ago. He was a very fierce man. He was conquering cities and provinces, one after another. The warlord was finishing sacking and burning yet another city. His men were killing or enslaving all the city dwellers who didn't flee before his army.

One of his senior officers reported to the warlord on the progress of the campaign in the city. This pleased the him. But when he heard that there was a monk who had refused to flee, and who was still staying in the monastery, he became enraged. Inflated with pride and anger, the warlord took a retinue of soldiers with him to visit the monk and kill him in person.

Striding up to the seated monk, he was furious that this skinny monk, alone, of all the remaining inhabitants in the city, was unaware of his might. He growled, *Don't you know who I am?* Without answering, the monk stayed unmoving, looking steadily at the warlord in all his bright armor.

The warlord, incensed at the insolence of this poor priest, this nobody, began drawing his sword, saying, *I can take this sword and run you through, without so much as blinking an eye.*

The monk calmly replied, *Don't you know who I am? I can sit here and allow you to run me through with your sword, without so much as blinking an eye.* The warlord, knowing that he had met his master, fell at his feet and became his disciple.

Commentary

It takes someone to bring flow into the system through embodying something new and fresh, to break the cycle of death and violence. Someone needs to have the willingness to live in the face of death, without being stopped by fear. Then things can change.

Horror

Death is ultimately, personal and faced alone. We wanted this book to be personal, as well. The following is my (Thomas) personal account.

We are very fortunate to have a highly skilled, colleagues group where we can explore our own personal material, experience how others are working and receive feedback on our own work. When I am a therapist working with a client, I often jump over the details of the trauma to avoid re-traumatization. And yet, at the same time, I also know that eventually, as Adyashanti has said, Consciousness comes back for everything, it will leave nothing behind. To me, this means that eventually, in order to finally be free of it, that I would have to become more intimate with the field of the trauma than one would ordinarily choose. As a client, I prefer a therapist who can help me to pace the process, to stay resourceful and yet to *leave no stone unturned*. The power that is inherent in finishing things completely, to be ruthlessly thorough, is part of the meaning of that expression.

And such therapists I knew I would find in my colleagues group as together, we have many years of deep and varied experience in systemic constellation and other forms of therapy as well as with spiritual practices. The complex, which I brought to the colleagues group to explore, was a life-long pattern of using eating as a coping strategy to reduce anxiety, particularly in social situations. From my previous plumbing of the inner depths, I hypothesized that the trauma related to the presenting behavior was probably quite old. And of course, eating is a biologically, core-level coping strategy.

Although I have a high level of trust and confidence in the colleagues group and have developed good personal resources, for two days before arriving at the meeting. I began to become aware of increasing nervousness in my body, like noticing how my leg was jumping up and down restlessly, or how I had unconsciously crumbled a piece of bread into dust.

It is common for a constellation to actually start before it appears to begin. The morning of a training or before a session, the therapist might be feeling things from the client field, emotions or sensations which will only come into context later in the day. Participants sitting in a constellation circle are sometimes in the role of a representative before the client has even come forward and the representatives chosen.

The dark side of my inner world

The first glimpse I had of the dark side of my inner world, was a repeating nightmare that had visited me much of my early childhood. It always started the same, with that familiar, sick recognition that I was back again, in that place of no escape, where nothing would erase the horrible scene and where I would never be safe. I was still too young then, still unaware of what humans are capable of doing to each other, to recognize the image for what it was - a killing field, the recent aftermath of slaughter.

In the dream, that boy who I thought I was, again was climbing over piles of recently slaughtered people, and feeling the dread in the pit of his stomach. With the fear came the knowing that the killers, the ones who could be seen there picking over the bodies, would notice that he was still alive. He must hold very still and pretend that he is dead too, but he knows that it will not work. In every dream they always find him. He must run! Get away! all the while knowing that they will catch him and butcher him too.

Each time I found myself in the dream landscape, I would try running, hiding amongst the bodies or somehow burrowing into the earth to escape. As a child, I favored places where I could hide, like a wild boar under a bush. A place where I could lie on sweet grass in the cool shade, in the darkness where I could see out, but not be seen. A place where I imagined safety and comfort. I imagined, that when I hid in the hole we had dug in the garden, that I could magically be transported to top of the pure, white mountain in the distance.

And only much later, would I have the resources to intentionally approach such a scene and stay present. Only in looking backwards, could I see how my presenting issue had a thread connecting it with the resignation and depression, which wound through my life.

In the nightmare, the resignation was that hopeless feeling that nothing beyond escaping would ever change things. Of course, in response, I developed extensive strategies for escaping reality. Now I realize, that while my desire for escaping was unconscious, it was exactly the correct initial step to make. Sometimes a strategic retreat to rally oree's sources is needed. Still, to actively take part in life, retreat needs to come to an end and eventually a course needs to be taken, or be forever reactive to circumstances.

The Constellation

The therapist suggested that we use a structural approach to working with the topic and asked that I choose three representatives: one for myself, one for the symptom, and a third to represent what lies behind it all. The man chosen to represent the presenting symptom acted as a barometer throughout the constellation. He stood to the side of the constellation and was only concerned that I stay present during the process. He became agitated if he felt that I was no longer present.

The woman in the constellation who was chosen to represent *what lies behind it all,* had already been in the role for some time before she was actually chosen for it. She had been fixated on how the anxiety that I was accessing, was showing in the way I kept one leg tightly wrapped around the other, like in some exotic yoga posture. The representative for me (Thomas) was lying on the floor. When the woman representative came in, my representative he stretched out an arm so that she could lie beside him. She lay down on the floor next to him for just a moment, when a look of abject horror took over her expression. She scuttled away hurriedly, hiding in terror under the table against the wall.

While the representative for me stayed lying on the floor, I was drawn into the constellation, putting my head near the floor and looking under the table at the representative for *What lies behind it all.* I said to her, *I see you. You are safe with me.*

She acknowledged me with her eyes and said, *I know.*

CUT

Slowly she came out from under the table and stood. Her look of terror subsided and she stood straight. She reported, I am not alone. There are many more here than just me. We have been beaten, raped, humiliated and hacked to pieces. But I am not afraid. It is all over. I am strong.

The therapist added two more representatives for my parents as resources for me. I stood by my father's side, looking at the representative for What lies behind it all. With piercing eyes and great dignity she looked directly at me, saying, I see you too. Thank you.will catch him and butcher him too. Each time I found myself in the dream landscape, I would try running, hiding amongst the bodies or somehow burrowing into the earth to escape.

As a child, I favored places where I could hide, like a wild boar under a bush. A place where I could lie on sweet grass in the cool shade, in the darkness where I could see out, but not be seen. A place where I imagined safety and comfort. I imagined, that when I hid in the hole we had dug in the garden, that I could magically be transported to top of the pure, white mountain in the distance. Unlike the thoroughness of Tamerlane, the genocide of Native Americans, which I encountered first in my dream world, was the destruction of an entire culture and way of life. But there is no escape for me into the innocence of the victim. My ancestry includes both the killers and those who were killed.

The woman in the constellation who was chosen to represent *What lies behind it all*, had already been in the role for some time before she was actually chosen for it. She had been fixated on how the anxiety that I was accessing, was showing in the way I kept one leg tightly wrapped around the other, like some exotic yoga posture. The representative for me was lying on the floor. When the woman representative came in, he stretched out an arm so that she could lie beside him. She lay down on the floor next to him for just a moment, when a look of abject horror took over her expression. She scuttled away hurriedly, hiding in terror under the table against the wall.

As the client, I was drawn into the constellation, putting my head near the floor and looking under the table at the representative for What lies behind it all. I said to her, I see you. You are safe with me.

She acknowledged me with her eyes and said, *I know.*

Slowly she came out from under the table and stood. Her look of terror subsided and she stood straight. She reported, I am not alone. There are many more here than just me. We have been beaten, raped, humiliated and hacked to pieces. But I am not afraid. It is all over. I am strong.

With piercing eyes and dignity she looked directly at me, and said, *I see you too. Thank you.*

Commentary

In this history, there is no escape for me into the innocence of the victim. My ancestry includes both the killers and those who were killed. Violence, killing those who are different, using sex as a form of dominance – these inherited histories stored in the inner library, are ironically, the very things which have lead me to peace, because they would not let go until they were integrated and had a place in my heart. When I close my heart to anything, it is too painful. I am the one who pays the price of having a closed heart. A Sufi master once said, All of the vast universes are contained in the tiniest corner of an open heart. I am an individual and the collective, both and beyond...

And Beyond...

I am the one whose heart was pierced by the sword. I am the earth which received my falling body, watered by my own blood and tears. I am the one whose hands held the sword. It was I who sexually dominated and then mercilessly cut those who were less than human. I am the very sharpness of the blade that was used to mutilate and take body parts as trophies. I am the corpse, sightlessly gazing at the sky. I am the raven eating the dead flesh from my own face. I am the hungry ghost searching for peace, and I am the wind which guided me home, to the refuge of my own heart. I am the landscape, returned to peace. I am the one who remembers, and the one who forgets. I am the silence that has always been there. I am the night sky. I am all of that, and none of that.

Falco biarmicus Ursula Franke